CW00435112

OUT OF THE DARK CLOSE

Scenes from a Glasgow Childhood

James Fitzpatrick

Kindle Direct Publishing

Copyright © 2020 Joëlle Fitzpatrick

All rights reserved

No part of this book may be reproduced, or stored in a retrieval system, or transmitted in any form or by any means, electronic, mechanical, photocopying, recording, or otherwise, without express written permission of the publisher.

Cover photograph courtesy of Mirrorpix.

CONTENTS

ACKNOWLEDGMENTS

My family and I would like to express our thanks to my late husband's dearest friends, Rob and Beth Robertson, for editing his memoir as well as Jamie Robertson for helping to prepare the paperback for publication.

Jim wanted to celebrate the amazing capacity of children to overcome the most difficult situations by finding joy and happiness in their imaginations.

He would have been delighted with the result, and on his behalf, we thank Beth, Rob and Jamie from the bottom of our hearts.

Joëlle Fitzpatrick

FOREWORD

I met Jim during the long hot summer of 1976. We were working in a hotel near Inverness during our university vacations, and we shared a cramped and shabby caravan in the hotel grounds. We also shared a love of literature, and an understanding born out of the experience of growing up in central Scotland in the '60s and '70s. It was the beginning of a wonderful friendship which only ended with Jim's untimely death from cancer in 2018.

Jim was a remarkable man. Deeply thoughtful, witty and loving. When he sensed that time was probably going to be short, he wrote a memoir recounting his childhood in Glasgow. Modest and self-effacing, Jim had not talked much about his childhood with his three children, and through this memoir he sought to share that experience with them.

The following pages reveal a mind which was both inquisitive and reflective. They offer a fascinating insight into the imaginative life of a young boy developing his own personality, and making the very most out of a challenging environment.

As social history, Jim's memoir recreates a rich picture of the Glasgow of his childhood. It also demonstrates the power and importance of education, and its ability to create opportunities for those who embrace it.

Ultimately, this is a story of optimism, and a belief that the future can be a far better place than the present.

Robert J Robertson

November 2020

PREFACE

I sat down one day to try out Google Maps. I entered the names of the places where I was born and brought up. The street in the Gorbals where I first saw the light of day in 1955 no longer existed. Then I checked out the tenement building in the housing scheme in Easterhouse where I had lived from the age of four to eighteen, and found that it too had been demolished. The street name still existed, but 80% of the buildings had been radically renovated or razed to the ground. I discovered that the population of Easterhouse had fallen from over 55,000 then to only 8,000 today. Google Maps showed a blank green space where I and thousands of others had lived, worked, and been educated.

It was like viewing the ruins of a Roman arena, when the guide tells you to imagine the crowds which once gathered to watch gladiators in combat. But all you can see is a heap of stones and rubble. I decided at that moment to try to capture the life that I had experienced in this place which no longer existed. I also wanted to explore the influences on a working-class boy, brought up in a post-war environment, to understand how his young mind was formed and how he tried to overcome the trials and tribulations of everyday life.

In doing so, I sought to leave a record, albeit brief, selective and highly subjective, for my three children who were born and raised in France, so that they could better understand their father's childhood and their own Scottish roots.

'The past is a foreign country', as L.P. Hartley said, 'they do things differently there.' People grow old, but they keep their past deep within them. The following chapters are about a young boy coping with life in Easterhouse in the 1960's when people lived 'differently'. Above all it is an attempt to fill the hole in the Google Map.

I. THE CLOSE

We lived up a 'Close', which in Glasgow was the front and back entrance and the common stairway which ran up through the tenement. All the tenement blocks in the gigantic East Glasgow housing scheme of Easterhouse were three stories high. All except one in Lochdochart Road, and that is where we happened to live. It had four stories and three flights of stairs, and naturally we lived on the fourth floor. Having a flat on the top floor was not a choice or a privilege. There was certainly no penthouse view and no lift. Being on the top landing meant that you came from the bottom of the pile. You were put there. Everyone wanted to be on the second or third floor, and some families were glad to be given a ground-floor flat - despite the noise at the entrance to the Close - as they had a patch of grass, which they could call their 'garden'. Nobody wanted to be in our flat and I understood why. I spent my childhood going up and down those stairs, never knowing what I would meet on the way.

Going up the stairs, I often used to hum songs of the moment which resounded in the darkness. Our teacher, Miss Markey, had like millions of others fallen under the spell of Julie Andrews in the box-office hit *The Sound of*

Music. She had taught us the songs. So, I would stride up the stairs, my chin held high, humming 'Climb every Mountain'. Later, when my tastes had changed and Robert Plant had replaced Julie Andrews, I would hum 'Stairway to Heaven'. That's where I was going, I imagined. I was on a Stairway to Heaven. But when I arrived at our front door, I always hesitated as I reached for the doorknob, particularly when I heard my parents arguing. At such moments my cheerful humming stopped, my heart sank and I knew I was not at Heaven's door.

On the way down, after the Sunday afternoon film on TV, which was usually a Hollywood musical, I would do a Fred Astaire light-stepping shuffle, or a snappy Gene Kelly kick and twirl at each landing. But sometimes I would recall the priest's threatening words at mass, warning us that we were all on a 'Stairway to Hell', condemned to a dreadful fate. The Close was a passageway, sometimes dark and sometimes light, reflecting my changing moods.

One of my earliest memories was when I was about four. I was unfamiliar with the stairs and landings, as we had just arrived in Easterhouse. I went out onto the landing to start the long descent, one step at a time, fumbling nervously along the wall to keep my balance. Suddenly it seemed to me that the Devil was coming to get me, just as Father Kelly had warned. The monster coming up the dimly-lit stairs had a gigantic hump on its back. Its head was bowed, and its face was hidden, but I saw its glinting swivelling eyes as it lumbered upwards, snorting and grunting. Its red tongue was covered in spittle and stuck out like a lizard's. I screamed in terror. The sound reverberated throughout the tenement. The Devil approached, ready to swallow me up. Doors opened, voices shouted, "What's up?" and "Who the hell's that?" Then the Devil spoke: "Oot the way son, will ye?" It was the coal man, the poor man who had to struggle up the stairs with a hundredweight of coal on his back. He side-stepped me and tipped the contents of his sack into our coal cellar on the landing. His shoulders heaved, and he twisted and rubbed his neck. My mother came out and paid him, and then shut the door, not noticing me cowering on the stairway with a bottled-up blubber on my lips. She obviously hadn't heard my scream, unlike the other neighbours. The coal man brushed past me, giving me a big comforting smile which shone brightly in his filthy face. I watched him go, leaving a trail of soot, and heard him reassure the neighbours that it was "only a wee boy howling up the stairs for his mammy." He wasn't the Devil. He was as dirty as the coal he carried, but he was bringing us fire and heat and light.

A lot of my childhood was made up of such moments, full of misunderstandings and mistakes, wild imaginings and unfounded fears.

Most people don't realise - or they forget - that stairs and landings can be frightening places for young children, especially in winter when it gets dark very early, or when the stairway lights don't work. Even with the lights on, there were ominous elongated shadows creeping along the walls as unseen strangers approached with heavy steps and heavy breathing. I would go up and down the stairs, holding my breath, groping the air ahead with one hand and leaning on the wall for reassurance with the other. I felt the presence of "the Bogey Man", the nasty figure that adults would joke to us kids about. They said that his favourite hunting grounds were dark Closes, and that their favourite victims were small boys on their own. For me, there were Bogey Men everywhere. My own father was one, like all the neighbouring men with one or two exceptions: scary, evil-smelling creatures, especially when drunk.

Although our Close could be dark and intimidating, it became a second home in many ways, as I felt on familiar ground once I got to know the neighbours. There were eight families up our Close. My Da separated them into two categories: Protestants and Catholics. We were natural allies with the Nolans on the third floor because they were the only other Catholic family. Da grudgingly tolerated the Protestant neighbours because he had to live beside them, and it was better not to make enemies. But secretly he hated them all, particularly Mr. Anderson who lived on the ground floor. A fervent Protestant, he had planted orange lilies in his front garden. According to my Da this blatant reference to the Protestant Orange Order was sheer provocation. I never knew if it was Mr. Anderson or my father who was the problem.

Our downstairs neighbours, the Lynch's, were constantly quarrelling; Mrs. Lynch was highly-strung and always in a bad mood. I kept away from them. Our next door neighbours, the McFadyens, had two little girls even younger than me. They were quiet and nice, and I felt at ease with them when I met them in the landing. Da despised Mr. McFadyen, probably because he was always sober, clear-eyed and never went to the pub. And Mr. McFadyen obviously disliked my Da, because he was the opposite. My Ma liked to gossip most of all with Mrs. Hamilton who lived on the ground floor. I liked Mrs. Hamilton just as I liked the Nolans; they clapped me on the shoulder when they saw me and smiled, and spoke to me, unlike most of the other adults who simply brushed past as if I were just a smudge on the wall.

All these families meant endless comings and goings on the stairs and landings with everyone bumping into one another. And the commotion was made worse as everybody was carrying something; mothers with shopping or prams, children with schoolbags or balls, or holding the hands of younger brothers and sisters.

When I was older and had my bike I had to carry it up the three flights of stairs and put it into our coal-shed so that it wouldn't get stolen. Carrying a bike up three flights of stairs was an arduous task for a small boy, like swimming against the tide while holding a suitcase. The wheels spun round with a will of their own and bumped against the stairs and my face, the handlebars swivelled round and belted my ears, and the chain dripped oil on my trousers as I struggled upstairs. I groaned when I met one of the neighbours coming down with young children and a basket of washing. Worst of all was when our big neighbour's son, Tam Lynch, came out of his door on the third floor with his huge 27inch bike. We passed each other like elephants trying to squeeze through a narrow doorway. Being much older than me, Tam had the right of way, and I always had to back up against the wall with the brakes of the handlebars stuck up my nose, trembling with the effort of holding onto my bike, while he barged past, muttering about 'bloody weans' getting in his way.

One good thing for us kids who lived on the upper floors was that we were allowed to howl up to our mothers from the backyard, to ask them to throw us what we needed, which was generally food. And the delicious Glasgow speciality for ravenous young children living in tenement blocks was a 'piece and jam' (or 'jeely piece'), which was two slices of bread with a dollop of jam inside - and butter if you were lucky. As soon as one of us started to shout for something to eat, everybody else did the same. An incredible din would start with all the kids yelling in sing-song voices "Maaamy! Maaamy! Gie's a piece..." Like quacking ducks, excited at bread being thrown to them, we stood with open mouths and outstretched arms, as our mothers threw down paper bags of food.

At the weekend, it was the other way round: Ma would 'do the messages'; shopping for food for the week ahead. She would call up to me to come down and help her. I would fly down the stairs like Superman and bring up the heavy bag, laboriously, step by step. I always felt proud 'lugging up' that big bag and I didn't want anyone to help me - which my big brother greatly appreciated. When I got to our landing, wheezing and gasping for breath, I felt like I had climbed Everest. Ma had rheumatoid arthritis and struggled to carry anything heavy or do some of the household chores like wringing out the washing. So, as well as carrying the 'messages' up the stairs and getting the coal for the fire, turning the mangle to squeeze the water out of the wet laundry was one of my other jobs after school. My aunt Netty was always getting on at my Da to get him to exchange our fourth floor flat for one on the ground floor or the first floor so that Ma didn't have to climb all those stairs, day in and day out, but Da typically took no heed of what she said. He wasn't one for change, at least not when it didn't concern him personally. It was too much of an effort for him. Ma's health didn't seem to concern him.

As I grew up, the stairs presented a marvellous challenge, at least when descending. Having mastered going down one step at a time, I began to jump the last two, then three, then four. I was Zorro, Spiderman and Action Man rolled into one. From four steps, I soon progressed to five, then six...seven...and finally, to my own astonishment and pride, to eight. On landing like a ton of bricks, I generally rolled over and crashed into the cellar doors while killing three Bogey men with my sword. Sometimes the neighbours, particularly Mrs. Lynch, came out to scold me, but I was already on to the next flight of stairs counting the steps ahead of me - then I would leap. The neighbours soon got used to my thumping descents and chaotic landings. My pals and I had competitions, daring each other to jump from higher and higher steps. The clatter, commotion, jeering and hooting made a terrible racket. Mr. Anderson, the ground floor neighbour who got the worst of our deafening antics would swing open his door in a blazing mood, and we all had to scarper, leaving him swearing and shaking his fist.

Since the neighbours tried to spoil our fun as we tried to break our necks, there were calls for vengeance. I never felt happy with the subsequent pranks, but I went along with my pals, particularly as they were mostly older than me. There were different degrees of vengeance depending on our mood and how we regarded the neighbours that we chose to annoy. The least offensive was to exchange all the doormats. This made everyone flaming angry and led to arguments between the neighbours. Sometimes we would take all eight doormats and put them outside Mr. Lynch's door, who, although completely innocent, would appear to be the culprit - as if he would want to collect eight doormats!

We were more lenient with Mr. Anderson and Mr. Hamilton. We only practised the classic trick of tying their doorknobs together with washing line, knocking on both doors, then running away to a safe distance to laugh while they tugged at their doors swearing to skin us alive if they caught us.

A more dangerous variation around Guy Fawkes night was to play the same masterstroke with tied doorknobs, but to light up a couple of bangers after we had knocked on the doors, calling out: "Police! Open up!" The sound of the bangers going off was like a bomb exploding in the confined space of the landing. It must have shocked and terrified those who were behind the doors. I once overheard my Ma, who was hanging up her washing and gossiping with a neighbour, say that old Mrs. McBride had almost had a heart attack and that whoever did such things should be locked up! I slipped away, at once worried and yet proud that I had done something that could send me to prison.

The Close was a fundamental part of our world. It was both inside and outside. It was covered, so it protected us from the freezing drizzle of a Glaswegian winter - or summer, for that matter. It was a hidden place, where we felt we were at home whilst at the same time outside of our parents' supervision. It was where we learned about forbidden things, seen only by our giggling friends. That was where my pals and I took our first slurps of revolting cheap wine and where they took their first choking draws on cigarettes. My pal, Hogie, got a kick out of scribbling rude drawings and swearwords on the walls of our Close (but not his own). I didn't much like this, but I laughed uproariously all the same when he did them.

The Close was where we felt able to share hilariously cruel stories about everyone we knew - classmates, teachers and neighbours. We imitated our favourite TV stars and comedians, endlessly repeating their brilliant sketches and jokes. The Close was a place where we learned to be sociable and where we could challenge the rules. It was our own church, a dark hall for a sect of sinful, silly boys.

We made such a racket that the neighbours hated us hanging about the Close. They were forever telling us to go and play or go home if it was getting late. "You've no place here!" they would say, ending with the empty threat of calling the police if we didn't go. We would shift outside reluctantly, but within five minutes we had slipped back inside or gone to another Close where one of our pals lived. The neighbours didn't understand that while we wanted to be miles away from them, at the same time we wanted protection, as we were secretly terrified of what lay outside.

The Close was a place where my pals and I felt close together and secure. And it was also an opening - our chance to escape from the closed and stultifying minds of our parents and neighbours. The Close was a place of transition, a passageway through which we took our first steps from childhood to adolescence.

2. THE BACK

"I'm just going out the Back" I would say to Ma as I opened the front door and went downstairs to play. 'The Back' was the shared backyard for all the tenement buildings in our block. All the Closes gave onto the Back, a rectangle of rough grass with two areas in the middle for huge metal dustbins. There were ten Closes in our block: five leading on to the upper part of the Back and five leading on to our side on the lower part. We could go anywhere in the Back, but the bins separated it into two distinct areas: the upper and the lower parts. I generally stayed in 'our' part of the lower end where everybody knew everybody else. There were washing poles all around the tarmac perimeter of the Back. The grassy inner part was supposed to have been turned into vegetable gardens, but only Mr. Anderson had made an effort to try to cultivate one. He had put up a rickety wooden fence and sown cabbages and rhubarb, but on the whole, there was little difference between his weed-infested 'garden' and the rough grass covering the rest of the central part. The Back was where the women gossiped as they hung out their washing, the place where the children played, where everybody found out everything about everyone else. It was a kind of sanctuary like the inner courtyard of a castle. We felt safe there. It was 'ours'.

The unwritten rule was that the Back was reserved for the children who lived in the surrounding Closes. So my friends from school who lived in other streets didn't come into our Back. They were immediately seen as outsiders, and they sensed it, so they kept away without having to be told to do so. I did the same thing when I was in 'their' territory. I knocked on their door to ask if they wanted to come out, but we went outside to the streets in the front of their tenement block, and only very rarely and for short periods inside their Back, where, as an intruder, I never felt at ease.

So I played with the children in the nearby Closes at our end of the Back. There were a lot of children there at that time who had mental health issues and physical disabilities, some of which were very severe. Perhaps it was something to do with endemic alcoholism, or bad health care or the selection of the families which were sent to Easterhouse. There were three kids in particular who lived up the Closes at our part of the Back who faced real challenges. We liked them, but we never regarded them as boys like us. We called them 'spastics', a word which had no derogatory connotations for us back then. One of them had Downs syndrome. He shuffled and grunted, and when he became excited he laughed like a donkey, which made us all laugh as well. He tried to join in the games, but he would suddenly stop whatever we were playing at as if he were lost, and would start howling and crying. Most of the time, he just stood holding onto a washing pole, his sad eyes fixed on the ground and his mouth open like a fish out of water. We saw him as just part of our community. We accepted him as he was part of the Back.

Our downstairs neighbour, Mrs. Hamilton, had two healthy children who were younger than me, David and Ann, but her eldest child, Thomas, had severe physical disabilities. He was very thin with a long face. His left arm hung limply, his paralysed hand drooped, and he staggered and wobbled as his legs were twisted and mis-shapen. He tried to join our simple games like tag, but he always ran out of steam after a few frantic bursts of run-ning. Then he would withdraw into himself and stand motionless like a twisted statue.

Then there was William. He was older and taller than most of the other children. Like Thomas, he was thin with a horse-like face and his mouth constantly frothed with saliva. He had a strange ungainly way of tripping about with one hand flapping like a dead fish. William always wanted to join in our games, and even though nobody really wanted him in their team, we always in-cluded him. He ran wildly after the ball when we played football, but he never seemed to know which side he was on or which goal to aim at. He loved dribbling with the ball, but often ran into the washing poles, which made us all laugh because usually he didn't hurt himself. But sometimes he lost control and did stupid things like run-ning into a wall which meant that he was always covered in cuts and scars.

These boys were never shunned or given special treatment. Perhaps we accepted them all so readily and let them play with us as we felt deep down that we were also outsiders. We were not at all like those smartly-dressed, pink-cheeked, well-spoken children who appeared on *Blue Peter*, which I watched every day after school.

The Back was our playground where we played all sorts of games. 'Kick the can', a variant of 'hide and seek' involved everyone, unlike football which was boys-only. The girls liked 'kick the can' as they could often run faster than the boys and were better at swerving to avoid being caught. On Summer evenings, after everyone had eaten their 'tea', we would all come out to play, and the Back would resound to the shrieks of the girls as they dashed out of the Closes to kick an old tin can which 'released' all the 'prisoners' who had been caught. Then everyone would run and hide while the poor kid designated 'it' would put the can back in place before setting off to find us. And then we'd chant from our hidey-holes all over the Back:

"Hunt, Hunt, Hunt for your men!

Hunt, Hunt, you lazy wee hen!"

And whoever was 'it' would demand: "Come oot, come oot wherever you are......!"

We also played rounders, a version of baseball. Two teams were lined up, one batting and the other fielding. The bat was a wooden table leg and the ball was made of soft rubber or rags and string, bound up to form what we called a 'clootie-ba'. No hard ball was allowed as it could have smashed a window. Most of the time the batsman swiped the air wildly and missed the ball, but every so often he would miraculously send it skywards, sending his team running around the pitch to marked points. This created an incredible moment of tension and screaming as the fielders ran about to retrieve the ball and bring it back to hit one of the four 'stumps'. Everyone cheated, as the batting team never truly respected the round they had to run and the fielders always hindered the players running. All this led to yelling and screaming which angered the touchy neighbours like Mr. Anderson who started roaring at us to give him some peace. What the adults didn't know was that the screaming and hooting meant that we felt safe and secure, caught up in the excitement of the game. They should have been more concerned when we went silent; it usually meant we were on edge having spotted outsiders lurking in the Closes.

The mixed games with the girls were always the most boisterous and joyful, but most of the time the girls and the boys lived separate lives. The girls stood huddled together whispering and giggling, or hopping and skipping. They often played hopscotch with a shoe-polish tin which they slid into chalk-marked boxes they had drawn up. This looked more like an elegant dance than a game, as the girls would twirl about with their arms held high stepping lightly from one foot to another. They seemed as obsessed with skipping as I was with keeping a ball in the air. Some of the girls could skip extremely well and do all kinds of elaborate moves with their skipping ropes, crisscrossing their arms and changing their steps. We secretly admired them and had to admit that the girls had an incredible sense of timing and control which was particularly evident when they skipped together. Two of them would hold up a skipping rope and start turning it high and fast, and the other girls had to jump in and skip to the beat. Sometimes three of them were skipping and 'birling' around inside the rope like circus performers. What puzzled me about skipping was the fact that it was strictly reserved for girls according to the rules of the Back. Any boy skipping would instantly be laughed at and called a 'sissy'. And yet our favourite boxer, Mohammed Ali skipped for hours in his training sessions. I secretly tried to skip, unseen in my room, pretending to be Mohammed Ali 'dancing like a butterfly and stinging like a bee'. I then realised how difficult it was as I got my legs tangled up in the ropes. In any case, our neighbour Mrs. Lynch, didn't appreciate my dancing like a butterfly and soon started hammering on her ceiling and shouting at me to stop my racket.

Apart from football and our war games, where we spent hours and hours slaughtering each other with imaginary weapons, we played a lot of hand games. One summer I became obsessed by 'Five Stanes' - a game I later discovered was played by the Romans. You threw a stone in the air from the back of your hand, picked up another, then caught the first stone in the air as it came down, and continued until you had achieved it with five stones, which wasn't easy. Three or four of us would sit on our haunches and play it in turn for ages. We were like those Roman legionnaires whiling away the hours with nothing but a few stones picked from the ground.

Another hand game was marbles which we called 'bools'. We went through crazes for weeks playing it, adapting the rules and the game to wherever we were. If we were beside a wall, we instantly developed all kinds of rules about how near to the wall you had to roll your 'bools'. Or if there was a manhole, which we called a 'stank', we would roll our 'bools' onto the pattern stamped on the round iron cover, with the depression in the middle being the main target. Marbles were made of glass with a coloured flame-like piece in the middle, and each had a value depending on its size and colour and whether it was new, chipped or cracked. The most prized were the huge ones we called 'conkers'; there were very few of them around. Our craze for the game set a fashion, too. The more 'bools' we had in our trouser pockets, the better we thought we looked. So, everyone started filling up their pockets to bursting point which made us waddle like penguins.

Knives were always present at that time in Glasgow because of the gang culture, so one of our favourite games was 'knifie'. This was a game where you stood with your feet apart, facing your opponent who threw a knife to stick in the ground by your feet. You then moved your foot to where the knife had landed and threw it back to where your opponent stood, putting him in an awkward, unbalanced position with his legs spread apart. There were elaborate rules about angles and the direction of the knife, and inevitably wayward throws led to injuries to legs and ankles. The girls would often come over to watch and bet on who would win. So we had to impress them which meant taking risks, usually resulting in blood and tears. And that's what the girls liked the most. They would roar with laughter when we cut ourselves, and run away, calling us stupid 'dopes'. They were right. We should have taken up skipping instead.

We exploited everything which the Back offered, making up games which were usually about daring each other to accept challenges. At the back end of each Close was a porch. We would clamber up and dare each other to walk around its edges on tip-toe or blindfold. And then we had to jump off as far as we could.

The washing poles were an endless source of inspiration for our games. When the women hung up their washing the flapping wet sheets prevented us from playing on 'our' poles, but otherwise they were our trees, trapezes, and the masts of our galleons. We would swing on them like apes, or writhe around them like boa constrictors. We had mad races where we had to swing three times around the pole to gain momentum and launch ourselves as far as possible, and then run and jump onto the next pole, and so on all around the perimeter. It was exhausting, and pretty dangerous, especially when the poles were wet as we could easily slip and crash to the ground. The poles were also great for tying up our captured enemies when playing Cowboys and Indians. We would torment our poor victims, lashing them with imaginary whips. Sometimes an adult would ask us what on earth we were doing. The answer was always the same: "just playing."

The Back was a funny kind of world where private matters were made public. The washing on the lines revealed everything about us, from the state of our underpants to the holes in the bed-sheets. Everyone was aware of everyone else's troubles, either through gossip or by witnessing the uproar when there were rows. Our games were regularly interrupted by shouting and the sounds of things breaking. This meant one of the neighbouring couples was having a fight. We'd hear foul language, murderous threats and, sometimes, the sound of scuffling and blows which meant it was serious and the police might come, which made it all the more dramatic.

One of the worst for arguing was Mrs. Lynch, our downstairs neighbour. She had a terrible temper and was always screaming at her poor husband who seemed placid to me, with his big bony face and monstrous ears. But Mr. Lynch was not the only target for fiery Mrs. Lynch. One day she was hanging out her washing when Mrs. Nolan, her next door neighbour, also came out with her washing. Some words were exchanged and then we heard Mrs. Lynch shouting insults at Mrs. Nolan, telling her to keep her eyes off Mrs. Lynch's husband. Mrs. Nolan retorted something about Mr. Lynch preferring to look anywhere, even into the toilet pan than to look at Mrs. Lynch's porridgy face. Mrs. Lynch's eyes blazed and she pounced on Mrs. Nolan, grabbing her by the throat and scratching her face with her fingernails. Soon they were rolling around in the muddy puddles, punching, kicking and scratching, while screaming vicious threats and swearing at one another. I had seen many boys fighting, but never anything like this. Not only did they hit each other with clumsy swipes of their fists, but they tried to bite each other's ears and stick their fingers into each other's eyes. Fortunately the neighbours came rushing out to separate the bedraggled, bloodied women with their dishevelled hair and torn clothes. Mrs. Lynch was hysterical and kept screaming and hurling insults, but Mrs. Nolan stood motionless with her head bowed as if in a state of shock. Mr. Hamilton, Mr. Anderson and Mr. McFadyen kept Mr. Nolan from becoming involved while Mrs. Lynch screamed that she wasn't finished. What I couldn't understand was Mrs. Lynch going on about that "dirty bitch", eyeing up her husband. Who on earth would look at Mr. Lynch with his big nose and cauliflower ears? And the women, too, were anything but alluring in their aprons and headscarves. They were just 'Mrs. so-and-so'; mothers, housewives, women who scrubbed the stairs, hung out the washing, carried shopping and young children in their arms. They weren't like the women in films, the gorgeous Rita Hayworth and Marilyn Monroe. For me, *they* were women. How could a man 'eye-up' Mrs. Nolan, or Mrs. Lynch with her scowling, hen-like face and mousy hair? It was a mystery.

One of the most dramatic events of the year that took place in the Back was Bonfire Night. The preceding days were dedicated to forming raiding parties to find, 'borrow' or steal any old pieces of wood: planks, old wooden crates, branches from nearby trees or old broken fences. Everything was thrown onto the bonfire pile which got bigger day by day. The only problem was raiding parties from other tenement blocks would come to steal our wood late in the evening when no one was about on those cold wintry nights. Whenever that happened, it meant retaliation. Everyone was summoned to invade a neighbouring Back under the leadership of one of the older boys, like Mr. Anderson's son Billy, who was a tough but calm and collected teenager. Like warring Indian tribes, we came back with our booty, whooping with pride.

On bonfire night, an older teenager or one of the men would light the bonfire as soon as it got dark. Many of the adults came down to see the bonfire and watch over the younger kids who were all very excited. There was a feeling of togetherness with children of all ages and their parents lined up around the fire with glowing faces. Chestnuts and potatoes were pushed into the hot ashes at the edge of the fire. A blackened half-burnt potato was delicious to eat in such an atmosphere with flickering yellow and white light dancing all around. The bonfire fascinated me, and I would find myself bewitched by the raging flames which were constantly whipped up by the older boys who threw on more wood or shook up the pile to air the fire. I loved how the fire changed all the time. I loved to see the flames rise up and curl in the night air, creating wild fantastic shadows and bursts of light. Smoke would pour out, then the fire would collapse into itself, only to start again all the more fiercely. It was alive to me, a living thing which breathed and moaned and then roared. My Ma or my brother would have to drag me away from the bonfire as the night drew on. Da disapproved of bonfire night; he called it a heathen Protestant ritual. I didn't really understand, but it had to do with Guy Fawkes being burnt in effigy because he was a Catholic. The adults in our Back didn't seem to fuss about this and there was no Guy Fawkes dummy. Bonfire night was just an event to celebrate and bring people together. My embittered Da couldn't see the fire in the way I or the others saw it. He resented the bonfire whereas I saw it as something precious: it magically bonded people together.

Some of the men, like my Da, never set foot in the Back. They kept to themselves, holed up in their flats or drowning their sorrows in the pub. But my pals and I saw the Back as a place where we felt free and safe, a place where we had fun and we tested ourselves, where we felt part of something bigger than ourselves, which in my case was as important as the home I shared with my family. Despite the arguments, fights, insults and rivalry, the Back brought us all together. It was like the village green, where people congregated, especially the youngsters. It helped to prepare us to 'come oot!' of the Close - not to back away from the world, but to confront it.

3. BIKES

One of the greatest days of my childhood was when I got
a bike - a brand new bike! It was an eighteen inch model
which I had seen in a bike shop window in Bridgeton,
near the bus stop beside my Auntie Peggy's. I stood spell-
bound, gazing at it while we waited for the bus back to
Easterhouse, knowing that it was made for me. One day,
Ma forgot something which she had left at Peggy's and
went back, leaving me at the bus stop. I pressed my nose
against the shop window and contemplated my beloved
bike. As I stood there, two boys hardly older than myself
stopped beside me to look at the bikes and then went into
the shop. This spurred me on to do likewise so I timidly
pushed the door open, went up to the man at the counter and asked how much the bike cost. He looked me over
to see if I was serious or just wasting his time. I lightly
fingered the bike's handlebars like a pilgrim touching a
sacred statue. The man said £18. My face fell, and I felt
tears well up in my eyes.

"How much have you got?" he asked, and then added,
on seeing my distress, "You know, we've got some other
bikes. Cheaper ones."

I thought of all my savings, representing months of

self-denial. I had somehow managed to save up all my pocket-money and birthday presents of postal orders, by converting it all into savings stamps which I religiously bought every week at the Post Office and stuck with glorious satisfaction in my savings book. These children's savings stamps weren't like ordinary stamps showing the Queen's grave and solemn profile. They showed a young boy, a cheery, bright, red-cheeked boy, brimming with the joy of having money. He was the image of myself. Sometimes Ma would borrow my savings book on a Wednesday when she had run out of money, and she would cash in a few of the stamps to buy milk or cigarettes. Fortunately, she always kept her promise to pay me back on the Friday when she got her own pay packet or my Da's. I had managed to save up over £3, which seemed like a fortune to me. But this, I discovered, was nothing compared to the price of the bike.

"£3....£3.10 pence." I mumbled, shuffling my feet, "I don't have enough". The man sniffed, and asked "What about your parents?"

"No," I replied, "They've got nothing. My ma even borrows from me sometimes."

"Let me show you some other bikes we've got," the man suggested, "Second-hand ones." I stood motionless, my heart set on *my* bike - the red one.

"What about your dad?" the man continued, and then he asked an odd question "Does he have a job? I mean, a regular job?"

"Aye." I replied hesitantly, not really knowing what job my dad did. "He goes to work every day and he comes back at tea-time, well, usually. Sometimes, he's on night-shift."

"Tell him to come round to see me. You bring your £3 - sorry, £3 and 10 pence - and we'll try to work something out."

My heart leapt, "You mean I could get the bike?"

"If you bring your mum and dad...maybe. We'll see."

I dashed out and ran to beg Ma to convince Da to come to the shop. My desperate pleading worked. The following Saturday, the three of us went to the shop. It felt strange as I had never before found myself walking outside with both parents. That was just not done at that time. We never went anywhere together.

I had been the model child all week and had worked on Da's sense of pride, telling him that it would make the neighbours' children jealous to see me on a new bike. I cashed in my savings stamps with mixed feelings of joy and regret, and gave the money to Ma, as she was the one who looked after money matters.

The man at the bike shop spoke to my parents, and soon I saw nodding heads. I was thrilled. I was to put down the first cash deposit with my savings and my parents were to pay the rest through a hire purchase scheme. I didn't know what hire purchase meant. All I saw was Ma handing over the money - my money - to the man, and Da signing a form. Then the man went into the shop window and wheeled out the bike, tested the brakes and chain, and gave it to me saying "the rightful owner!" I took it by the handlebars and carefully wheeled it out of the shop, feeling like the cheery boy on the savings stamps. I was beaming with the joy of possessing my greatest desire. I had my own bike. It was fantastic. It was bright red with brilliant chrome handlebars.

In fact I wasn't just buying a bike. I was buying a horse. A red horse. It was alive to me, and it was mine. I called it Thunder. As soon as I got it back home I took it outside into the Back to show it off to my pals who gaped with envy and awe. I naturally fell off the first few times as my short legs were stretched to their limits at every turn of the pedals, making me slouch from one side to the other, with my buttocks rolling awkwardly on the saddle and my fingers gripping the brakes. Soon, however, after one of the older boys had adjusted the saddle to suit my legs, I was doing the round of the Back. This meant cycling hard up the slope on the left to wheel round the straight bit at the top, and then turn to come down the other side with a final steep dip and a screech of the brakes between the washing poles. With every round my confidence increased, and soon I was even beginning to look where I was going as I rattled forward to the alarm of mothers and their wandering toddlers. I was in my element. I was an Apache warrior called 'Fleetfoot' and I was galloping through the Grand Canyon under a sweltering sun with billowing sand blowing behind me. My horse, Thunder, flew like the wind, neighing and snorting, unstoppable but still attentive to my every command. We leapt over rocks and rivers and I shot dozens of mighty bison and nasty 'white settlers'. My pals ran after me, begging me to give them 'a shot' on my bike.

Perhaps influenced by my brand-new bike, all my pals

managed to get hold of a bike in the days that followed - either through an older brother handing over an outgrown one, or by acquiring a second-hand one - and we all fell into a bike craze. After school, and at the weekend, we became bike-mad and whirled around the surrounding streets like a pack of yelping dogs. Having mastered my faithful steed, I started to show off by riding fast with only one hand on the handlebars, trying to look nonchalant by letting my free hand dangle limply at my side. Then it was no hands at all. There were wobbly beginnings and a few falls and scrapes, but soon we were all striving to outdo one another and ride with no hands for as long as possible. With mindless recklessness, we adopted the logical next step of riding with our eyes closed. We all cheated at first and left our eyes open a slit, but then being crackpots, we did actually try to ride blindfold. This, of course, led to near fatal falls due to the bumps and potholes in the road which sent the front wheels at all angles. Our bikes were soon battered and scraped, but somehow to us small boys, this was a sure sign of our intrepidness. So just as we beamed with joy on the first day's outing with a clean and shiny bike, so we became proud of the scratches; these were like medals for our daring.

Ma didn't see things that way, however. "What have you done to your bike?" she shouted at me one day, enraged at seeing the terrible state it was in. ""We've just bought it!"

"I was just playing, Ma." I answered sheepishly, "I fell off."

"The man at the bike shop will be furious." she replied,

"He'll never take it back!"

I then discovered what hire purchase meant. The bike didn't actually belong to us until my parents had paid off the final instalment. If they couldn't pay, the bike went back to the shop. If it was damaged, it lost all its value.

"But you won't stop paying the instalments." I argued.

"Who knows what'll happen." She answered grimly, "Your Da could be laid off...or be out on strike."

"When is it mine?" I asked desperately, and added, "I mean, ours...completely."

"Next year." Ma sighed, "The instalments won't be over for another twelve months."

Twelve months seemed like an eternity. Nevertheless, I decided, just in case, to treat my bike more gently. I promised Ma to be more careful and led Thunder away to heal its wounds.

My imagination helped me to resolve the problem. My bike had magical properties. When I found myself alone it transformed itself into whatever my mind fancied. When I was on Thunder, my horse would wear a thick leather coat to protect it from arrows or bison horns. And when my trusty Thunder had to rest and sleep after bison hunts my bike changed itself into an Aston Martin (after seeing James Bond in *Goldfinger*) or a Spitfire (after building an Airfix model of one). Naturally I protected it with thick invulnerable armour-plating to ward off enemy bullets. I often turned it into a motorbike with a deep throbbing engine which growled warmly and roared when I twisted the handlebars. I was Steve McQueen in *The Great Escape,* scrambling over muddy fields, a squad

of German bikes hot on my tail, firing machine-gun sal-
voes. Going down hill, the wheels of my bike became a
pair of skis and the handlebars my ski-sticks. I slid down
from the top of Mont Blanc, leaping over crevasses at
breakneck speed, starting avalanches as I swerved left
and right, and performing triple somersaults over pine
trees. Going through the dimly-lit tunnel under the railway bridge which was full of trash and puddles, I guided
a nuclear submarine carefully through icebergs, avoiding
depth-charges exploding around me. When I emerged
into the cold daylight, I scanned the icy wasteland, and
whipping up my huskies, set off on my sledge, laden with
the fur of the grizzly bears I had shot, hoping to reach my
log cabin to light a fire before dusk, just in time to escape
from the wolves.

But swerving round lampposts and washing poles had
its limitations. And the streets in our neighbourhood
could not satisfy a group of fearless boys like us forever.
But we instinctively knew that we were confined to a
very few streets around our tenement block - that was
our territory. Most of the streets elsewhere were tacitly
out of bounds as they 'belonged' to the gangs who con-
trolled them. We could risk going into such no-go areas if
we were with a classmate who lived there, but a crowd
of us all together on bikes would be seen as provocative.
The unspoken rule was to respect such invisible borders.
We meekly did so. The solution, we realised, was to set our
sights further afield, outwith the surrounding gang territory. My pal Frank told us that his big brother had once
biked to the Campsie Fells to the north of Glasgow, all the

way there and back in the same day. Why shouldn't we? So, Frank found out from his brother how to get to Lennoxtown at the foot of the Campsies, and one Saturday morning when it wasn't raining, we set off. There were only five of us as some of my pals' parents didn't let them go. I had prudently not said anything about going anywhere. I sneaked out some bread and biscuits in a paper bag, and as I closed the door, I said that I wouldn't be home for lunch as it was a pal's birthday and his mother had invited us all to his place, and it would probably go on all afternoon.

Once past our streets we quickly sped through the territory of the 'Drummy', one of the Easterhouse gangs, and then found ourselves in the unknown. Frank muddled up his brother's directions and we were soon lost. We found ourselves on main roads with enormous trucks thundering past, making our bikes wobble and scaring the life out of us. Every road seemed to be uphill. "A good sign" Frank said, as that meant we were heading for the Campsies. We panted and struggled to peddle as far uphill as we could, then dismounted and wheeled our bikes with our chests heaving and gasping for breath. At every major crossroads we were bewildered and we often lost time going the wrong way and having to come back and take another road. Finally, however, after three hours of pedalling, our perseverance paid off and we reached the foot of the Campsies. We threw down our bikes triumphantly on the wayside and set to munching crisps, spam sandwiches and my biscuits.

When we had finished and taken a rest we looked

around, not quite knowing what to do now that we had arrived at our destination. We felt the emptiness that surrounded us was rather intimidating. The huge purple-black clouds looming above our heads sent gigantic ominously shifting shadows sliding across the surrounding hills. The boggy moor leading to the foot of the hills didn't look inviting either. On top of that, the last thing we wanted to do was walk. "It should be easier, going back. It'll be downhill this time." I said. "And it looks like rain…" Duffy, added with a frown. There was nothing more to say. We all felt the urgent need to escape from the wild atmosphere of the unfamiliar place. Once on our bikes, especially going downhill, we all cheered up and put the difficult moments of the day behind us. We were intrepid heroes, going back to base camp after a dangerous mission.

That was the first of many outings into the surrounding unknown. The first few times we retraced the route we had struggled to find leading up to the Campsies, and explored some of the nearby villages, like Milton of Campsie where we got off our bikes and walked around at the foot of the Kilsyth Hills. However, we never wandered very far as we were scared our bikes would get stolen, which would leave us in the lurch in the middle of nowhere. So our heads were constantly swivelling. Our attention was not so much focused on the wonders of nature, more on making sure our bikes were still in sight.

One Saturday we even managed to reach the town of Kirkintilloch. It seemed to us that we had gone all the way to New York, such was the difference between this place and our breeze-block housing scheme. It was a real town with old stone churches and winding cobbled streets, white cottages with blue window frames, nice-looking pubs and all kinds of strange shops with antique furniture and pottery in the windows. We wheeled our bikes around, but didn't dare go into any of the shops. We pressed our noses up against the window and pointed at the odd items on sale, like old agricultural tools, or at a fascinating shop selling real hunting rifles and knives. We sensed the shop owners glaring at us. We suspected they were getting ready to bar the way if we dared to open the door, as they had probably assumed that we were riff-raff; we were Glasgow urchins, which meant that we were shop-lifters. So we sat beside a burn under an old stone bridge and made fun of the local accent which we tried to imitate. If we were toe-rags to them, they were 'teuchters' to us.

We never really knew what to do when we arrived somewhere. Having no money to buy anything and having no idea what to look at, we kept our distance and glanced about the places we visited before moving on. There were exceptions, of course, like the outing we made to Uddingston where we discovered, to our excitement, a sign saying 'Zoo'. However, we soon found that we didn't have enough money between us to all get in. So we climbed up the fence and peered over to see what we were missing, hoping to catch sight of ferocious tigers, rogue elephants, and screaming baboons. What we saw was a pretty shabby affair, with a few gloomy camels, two dejected zebras and a lugubrious llama. They looked listlessly at us as we made silly faces at them and grunted stupidly. This brought one of the zookeepers out of a hut to tell us to clear off. And so we did, relieved not to have wasted our money on such a dump. We weren't bothered. Wherever we went we were met with hostile looks. No adult ever welcomed us. Being children, we seemed to be a problem for them.

My once shiny bike was getting more and more battered and scratched due to the punishment I inflicted on it during our outings, but it also suffered from other failings which I had to learn to handle. I discovered that my bike was not just an object, it was a machine made of many parts, some of which needed maintenance and repair. A few days after I acquired the bike I found my legs churning round and round as if they were pedalling in thin air, and then my bike finally slowed to a halt. To my consternation, I saw that the chain had come off the big cog of the chainwheel. I looked at it helplessly, thinking that I had broken the chain for good. Just then, an older boy called Big Shuggie came over and said kindly: "It's nothing to greet about." He upended my bike and showed me how to put the chain back on the cog. Then he gave the pedals a spin. The back wheel whirled round and I glowed with relief, thanks and renewed happiness. The following day it was my left brake which didn't work, making me skid all over the place. Again, Big Shuggie came to the rescue. He upended the bike, pointed out how the brakes were connected to the wheels through a wire, then fiddled about with the brake-pads until they closed perfectly on the rim of the wheel. He then explained how to use a multiple bike-spanner to loosen and tighten all the different nuts and bolts. It was an incredible tool, designed to fit all the different sized nuts on the bike. I handed it back deferentially, but he told me to keep it. "You can do anything with that" he said. I held it in my hand as if receiving the sword of Excalibur. "Get yourself a puncture outfit, too." he added. "A puncture outfit and a spanner, and you'll be all right, wherever you go." I felt great. I had discovered that machines broke down, but that you could fix them. I began to enjoy turning my bike upside down and checking that everything worked. Somehow my bike belonged to me in a different way. I was responsible for it working correctly. It was dependent on my care.

Big Shuggie was right: it wasn't long before I experienced my first puncture, which wasn't surprising, given all the broken glass littering the streets. This time it was my brother who fixed it. It was like watching a surgical operation. First of all, he took off the wheel and took it up to our kitchen. He used the handles of two spoons to lift the tyre out of the wheel-frame. Then he slipped out the valve and pumped up the inner tube and put it into a basin of water. Tiny bubbles appeared. "That's the puncture." he explained, "The air's coming out at that point." He dried the tube and marked the tiny hole with a square of chalk. I marvelled as he squeezed a blob of thick glue onto the hole, and put on a round rubber patch. After letting the glue take hold he re-inserted the tube and put the tyre back into the rim of the wheel, and finished by pumping it up. It worked. The puncture had been repaired. I insisted on putting the wheel back onto the front fork of the bike and tightening the bolts as if I had repaired the puncture myself. I felt I could face anything from then on, just as Big Shuggie had said. The following week I bought my own puncture outfit with my pocket money and put it into a small satchel attached to the back of the saddle along with my trusty spanner. I was armed for whatever I encountered on the road.

I was often put to the test as many mishaps came our way on our outings. There was always one of us who had a defective chain, a brake failure or, worst of all, a puncture. Then we all groaned as it meant we would be held back for some time. But fixing a puncture made us puffed up with pride and we always set off again in a good mood.

Through my bike I discovered there was a chain linking us together. When you had a problem, someone with more experience taught you how to fix it, and you became more independent. And you were able to pass on that knowledge to the younger kids. Whenever something bad happened to one of us, the others joined in to help out.

That's what I didn't understand about my Da. He was a skilled tradesman, a turner, and he had a big box of tools in one of the hall cupboards. But he never showed me or explained how things worked. Once, he had to put a new plug on a lamp, and I hung about to see what he was doing. He turned his back on me and did something with a screwdriver and a pair of pliers, then in a self-satisfied way, said "Give that to your mother." We were supposed to applaud. Da was one of those people who kept things to himself, perhaps to help him to feel superior. He never shared his experience. I didn't learn anything from him; I got it all from Big Shuggie, my pals and my brother. They were the generous ones. They passed on the parcel of knowledge. My father kept his little parcel all to himself. It was very sad.

Our bikes freed us from bus routes and train timetables. We pedalled wherever we wished. When we arrived, it was not just the destination which mattered, but also the sense of freedom which we enjoyed on the journey. Although I couldn't have articulated it at the time, I instinctively knew that life was about being in motion, becoming independent and taking risks. Bikes offered us all of that. My bike enabled me to explore on my own, lost in my own thoughts, or to be part of the group moving together. It was one of the stages of my childhood: I went from crawling to walking to running and finally to cycling.

Adults on bikes are a different species. They cycle for practical reasons or for exercise. Cycling for children is something else. It makes their minds whirl like the wheels of the bike. I had a bike which became a horse charging over the plain...a dolphin leaping and plunging through the ocean...a tank thundering through the desert with unstoppable force...a spaceship zooming through interstellar emptiness, heading for Mars.

I had a shiny red bike which became battered and scratched, as it took me far from the ugliness of Easterhouse to the best destination of all, my imagination, where the wheels of the mind went round and round... round and round...

4. FOOTBALL

Like many cities with strong working-class traditions, Glasgow was football mad. We were brought up to run after a ball like hounds on the scent of a fox. It was in our blood and we couldn't control it. Well, I couldn't. From morning till night I spent my childhood dribbling, kicking and heading a ball. Football is one of the few sports that don't really require any equipment - except a ball of sorts. It's the poor man's sport *par excellence*. Our goalposts were our jumpers or schoolbags. The boundaries of the 'pitch' were washing poles, pavement kerbs, fences or walls. The pitches themselves were set up anywhere: a car park, a backyard, a field, a playground. On most of the pitches I played on, not only did we have to dribble past our opponents, but we had to avoid washing poles, cars, postboxes and street lamps.

Our favourite 'pitch' was the swing park beside the local shops. The Council had deigned to build a playground for the likes of us with three swings, a roundabout and a slide. Within two days the swings had been ripped off and stolen. The iron roundabout and slide stayed put. It's hard to steal a roundabout riveted into slabs of concrete. In all the years I played football in that swing park I never once saw a mother with her toddler on the round-about or at the slide. I understand now. They must have been terrified at the sight of us lot running about wildly and kicking the ball as hard as we could off the round-about, taking it on the rebound, and swerving round our opponents. The iron posts which once held the swings were our goalposts. The local Council never bothered to replace them. So every day after school and at the week-end, in our minds the swing park became Hampden Park, Glasgow's gigantic football stadium, which could accom-modate up to 130,000 at that time. No one was watching us, but we felt we were all stars; as I ran about there was an endless football commentary playing in my head: "he's on the ball - the new tantalising wizard from Glasgow. He's soaring down the left wing, dribbling past one, two, three defenders..." and so on.

You soon learned your place in the world of football. Every game began by picking sides using 'tic-tac'. The two best players, the captains, faced one another as if they were in a Western shoot-out. They walked, heel to toe, one step at a time towards each other, and the captain who first trod on the other's foot was given first choice of the assembled hopefuls. Then the captains called out names alternately and you soon learned if you were the third, fifth, seventh best player...or one of the useless ones that no one wanted in their team. These poor kids, who were humiliated daily by being picked last, were never-theless necessary, as we needed teams of at least six players. So they were not ostracised. Indeed, they were ac-tually much appreciated for their lumbering inability to control a ball, as this made the rest of us look fabulously talented. We knew we could run rings around them and steal the ball effortlessly.

I was born with the lucky gift of being left-footed (while being right-handed). Everyone else I knew was right-footed and I found it easy to baffle them. And so the captains always chose me first. And when I was older, and became the dictatorial captain, I called out the names according to our cruel Darwinian system. Our goalkeepers were generally useless and only stopped a ball if you hit it straight at their stomach, leaving them doubled up in pain, gasping and winded. So goals were relatively easy to score. We had two kinds of game. To win you had to score eleven goals, or on Sunday when we had so much time to kill, we set the target at twenty-one. No wonder we were puzzled by the football results, religiously intoned on the radio at five o'clock every Saturday: "Hearts one...Rangers one; Falkirk one...Aberdeen nil". Our results were more like rugby scores: "Eddie's team sixteen...Wullie's team twenty-one".

Scoring a goal was the sole aim of the game and the path to glory. There were no tactics, no strategy, just bull-like charging up and down the pitch, dribbling frantically and only passing the ball to someone on your side if you knew you were about to lose it. Otherwise you held onto it as long as you could, and if you had a chance to score you struck out at the goal. We weren't really two teams so much as two groups of individuals playing against each other. The joy of scoring was deeply satisfying and thrilling. You were a warrior striking a killer blow. As important as scoring, was the way you did it. Most goals were shambolic. They involved frantic shoving and swiping at the ball which somehow found its way past the so-called goalkeeper. Headers were the worst. A leather ball hitting you on the ear or the back of your head left you stunned and reeling. It was like being hit on the head with a hammer. The ball would fly in any direction - and even sometimes into the goal. Occasionally there were magical moments when you hit the ball perfectly and it flew, as if carried by angels, into the top corner of the goal. Or someone actually managed a decent corner kick and you headed the ball with your forehead (for once), squarely into the back of the 'net'. These goals were acclaimed and celebrated - everyone rushed up, yelling their praise. Nonchalantly, you would play down your masterstroke. But secretly you were bursting with pride and delight.

When I was with one or two pals, we would spend hour after hour practising our skills; elaborate back heels, keeping the ball up with our knees, or heading the ball to one another in long 'keepie-up' sessions. We were acrobats performing amazing feats to the roar of the crowd. When I was alone, I would repeatedly head the ball off a wall, counting out loudly to impress any girl who might be passing: "forty-six...forty-seven...forty-eight..." Like a religious believer at the Wailing Wall, I would enter a trance-like state, though when I stopped I came back down to earth with a stiff neck and a head like a punch-bag.

My own little gang was composed of four close friends. First there was Mintsy, a thin, fair-haired, pale-faced boy who was good in class. We called him Mintsy because his surname was Murray, which made us think of *Murray Mints*. Then there was Gerald McDuff, or Duffy, who was tall for his age, dark-haired, and better off than the rest of us because his father was a commercial traveller who even owned a car. Peter Hogan, or Hogie, was fat, jovial and a bit slow in class. And then there was Terry Hughes, or Hughie, a quiet, shy boy who hardly said a word and who clung to us like a lost pup.

One day we decided to take ourselves a bit more seriously and do justice to the great game of football by saving our pocket money to buy Scotland team strips. Eventually we were dressed in baggy white shorts and dark-blue shirts, red and blue socks and football boots with real studs. Duffy's mum had even bought him shin guards. He soon regretted it as we all set about kicking him on the shins to test them out, while poor Duffy squealed and protested that he wasn't playing any more.

My mates unanimously proclaimed me manager and captain of the Scotland team. I told my team to line up behind me as I was going to lead them into Hamden Park to play against England. Tooting and humming the *Scotsport* theme tune, we solemnly entered the 'stadium' in our Back to the enthusiastic barking of Duffy's dog. We convinced a couple of kids - ones that were useless at football - to play against us. We thrashed them eleven-nil, and of course put it down to our brilliant play. Having routed the Sassenach enemy, we felt it fitting to award ourselves a championship cup, and to immortalise ourselves in a photo holding our trophy. Duffy was the only one whose dad had a camera so we persuaded him to borrow it, and one of his mum's shiny candlesticks to be the cup. One of the kids agreed to take a few snaps of the victorious Scottish team. As I was captain I held the candlestick triumphantly above my head as my loyal teammates stood beside me. In the next photo, the 'official' one, we lined up posing as stiffly as Scots Guards. Mintsy and I half-knelt in front with one hand on our knee and the other hand on our hip. Behind us, Duffy, Hughie, and his wee brother (whom we had roped in to make a five), stood proudly with their arms tightly folded over their puffed-out chests. We looked defiant and ready to take on anyone. We even re-enacted some of our glorious goals: I froze dramatically with the ball at my feet and Hughie gaped with amazement as he watched my lethal left foot, poised, about to score another cracking goal for Scotland.

If only the reality had been otherwise. Throughout my childhood Scotland was often beaten. And yet it didn't bother us. In our fantasy world we were invincible. Maybe our Scottish self-deluding optimism was a survival mechanism. We could endure defeat after defeat, and yet when the next game began we still believed that we were better than anyone else.

Someone told the manager of one of the local junior teams that I was a good player, and he told me to come along for a trial. I went along and was told to try to beat a couple of defenders around the penalty area and then try to score. I had ten minutes and scored five goals. I was picked for the team and soon became captain. We wore a red and white striped shirt and we played in a real junior league on pitches with real goalposts! There were eleven players in each team and I couldn't believe it - we even had a referee. As captain, I brought Duffy into the team and asked the rest of our friends to come and cheer us on and applaud all our goals.

However, my dreams of greatness were soon to be shattered. The next few weeks were full of disappointment. Every Saturday morning I encountered 'reality'. We were thrashed in every game: 8-1; 7-2; 9-1. I found some consolation in scoring a couple of goals, but most of the time I was picking the ball out of the back of the net and carrying it to the centre line, hissing "Get a grip, will you!" to my teammates, only to pick the ball out of the net again ten minutes later. Perhaps I was a lousy captain, but I discovered that the real problem was that our so-called 'manager' wasn't a real manager at all. He was simply a well-intentioned bloke who wanted to help kids like us by giving us something sociable to do to stop us from becoming delinquents. So, to my great dismay, I learned that he took on almost any kid, whether they were any good or not. I thought I had been selected for my extraordinary ball skills! There were only three or four of us in the team who took football seriously and could actually play. The others could barely tie their bootlaces.

Disheartened, I decided to quit the team but I realised that I couldn't return to the fantasy world in which I was a world-class genius. Things had changed. I had seen loads of youngsters in other teams, some even younger than myself, who could play much better than me. I might have been the best player in our team, but I clearly saw that I was just an average player compared to the boys with real talent. So at a still tender age I decided to 'hang up my boots', having encountered the cruel reality of the football hierarchy. I now knew what it felt like to be one of those boys who were the last to be chosen. However, I soon found fulfilment in another role. I was no longer the star. I became a follower of stars. I became a Celtic fan.

There was an invisible Berlin Wall through Glasgow at that time separating everyone into two tribes. If you belonged to the Protestant majority, you supported Rangers. If you were a Catholic, you supported Celtic. There was nothing really religious about it. It was just a fact of life. We were Catholics, so we were the 'Tims' with green genes and they were Protestants, the 'Huns' with blue genes, and we were told they were totally unlike us. I had the good fortune to become a Celtic supporter when they had their greatest manager, the visionary and pragmatic Jock Stein. Instead of playing like us and scrambling about for the ball, which some Scottish teams still did, he introduced tactics and strategy. Our defenders protected their half of the pitch and also moved up to support the forwards. Our midfielders dominated the play, our forwards anticipated passes, rather than simply running after the ball. It seemed effortless. It was beautiful to watch. It was football as it should be played.

From the age of ten I did all I could to get to the Celtic matches at Parkhead. My pals and I managed to scrape together enough money for the bus fare, but we never had enough for the tickets. Fortunately there was a tolerant attitude amongst the men, and one of them would give in to our pleading and give us a 'liftie-over' the turnstiles into 'Paradise', as Celtic Park is rightly called. Once inside, we would go to 'The Jungle' where the wild supporters gathered. As we were so small we had to clamber up onto the iron girders supporting the stadium in order to see the pitch. Once there, we learned everything we needed to know about the bigotry and vulgarity of the men, especially when they'd all had several pints. But we didn't mind. We joined in the stomping and chanting and the cheering and jeering. We were monkeys in 'The Jungle', hanging onto the girders and screeching with gleeful ecstasy. We screamed like Beatles' fans when the Celtic players came onto the pitch, and we exploded with joy when they scored. It was usually freezing or drizzling during the long winter football season and the wind ripped us raw, but we clung onto each other and shouted ourselves hoarse, barely noticing that we were shivering and soaked to the skin. Our hearts were on fire and we felt the spark of existence. We were witnessing the Beautiful Game performed by our very own team. It was magic.

After the match we went to the team exit and waited to see our idols, showered and wearing, to our surprise, plain clothes. We had thought that they always wore Celtic strips and boots, even in bed. We would run up to our heroes and breathlessly beg for an autograph. Generally they would very kindly take pity on the hordes of boys, and sign the bits of paper in our outstretched hands. I got them all: Jimmy Johnstone, Tommy Gemmell, Bertie Auld, Stevie Chalmers, Billy McNeil, Bobby Lennox, to name but a few. In my mind these autographs were coded messages containing the secrets of football, magic tokens which would empower the owner to play like these Gods. I cherished them and showed them off at school as if I were the personal friend of every member of the team. I gained in stature in the other boys' eyes. But I was bewildered to see that the girls only sighed, raised their eyebrows and turned their backs.

One of the highlights towards the end of my childhood, was the 1967 European Cup Final in Lisbon between Celtic and Inter Milan. It was played on a school day, but lessons were stopped in the afternoon and we were allowed to watch the match. The whole school gathered in the refectory and everyone's eyes, even the girls that day, were glued to the flickering screen. There was something otherworldly about it all to see 'our' players, men whose autographs we had collected, standing proudly as the national anthems were played, about to compete in the most prestigious of Cup Finals. One which no British team had come close to winning. Inter Milan played as the Italians did at that time, with defensive mastery, biding their time and then executing a lightning strike to score just one goal to kill the match. They showed total scorn for our Scottish heroes whom they kicked to bits behind the referee's back. We were driven mad by the injustice of it all. Inter were the obvious favourites and would be the certain winners. They only had to get through the ninety minutes before holding up the cup. It was a foregone conclusion.

Unlike in 'The Jungle' where we gave free rein to our emotions and screamed to our heart's content, at school we were tense and embarrassed. The teachers' eyes were upon us, and they hushed us when we expressed our fears and outrage. The tension increased as the match drew on into the second half with the score at one all. Already it had been a kind of victory for us as Celtic had scored. Our honour was secure whatever the final result. And then, out of the blue, the ball landed at Stevie Chalmers' feet in the penalty area, and he turned and scored: the winning goal! We could hold back our emotions no longer. We went berserk, rising to our feet to jump with joy, knocking over chairs, screaming and ignoring the headmaster's calls for silence.

Later in life, I read in George Orwell's essay, *The Sporting Spirit,* that 'serious sport has nothing to do with fair play. It is bound up with hatred, jealousy, boastfulness, disregard of all rules and sadistic pleasure in witnessing violence: in other words, it is war minus the shooting'. I couldn't agree more; that is what I experienced as a child. We hated our opponents, we were jealous of any player scoring against our team, we were full of boastfulness whenever our team scored. We lied and cheated and had a total disregard for rules, and we did take a sadistic pleasure in witnessing violence when one of our favourite defenders crunched his boot into some forward's right foot. Yes, it was 'war minus the shooting'.

But it was a lot more than that; there were so many emotions at play. The thrilling expectation and growing excitement before the match, the pride and respect we felt as our team entered the pitch, the sound of the national anthems, and the tension, fear and disappointment when things went badly. And of course the delight, joy and relief when things went well. It was exhausting. But most of all we'd been sharing an experience, a wonderful experience that brought everyone together.

In football I saw the worst and the best of human exchanges. Everything turned on that little ball dancing at our feet which had such an impact on the other little ball in our heads. When I entered year 6 at the age of twelve, the English teacher told us to read *MacBeth*, probably because it was a Scottish play. I was struck by the line 'Fair is foul, and foul is fair'. I saw the foul and the fair in supporters, and in great players, and it taught me about the foul and the fair in myself. Yes, kicking a ball about in the back streets of Glasgow was probably one of the best ways for a child to learn about the fair and the foul in life.

5. NAMES

When I was around two or three I realised that I had a name. I was called Jim. I was unique. My brother was a different person. He was called John. But when I went to school at the age of five I discovered that my name wasn't Jim, but James. I found that strange: at home I was Jim, at school I was James. I felt that there were two of me, and I changed depending on where I happened to be. Then I learned that my Da was called James, too, like me, and my grandfather who was dead, but who looked at us from a photo, was called John like my brother. Then I found that my great-grandfather on my mother's side was called James, like his father before him, and on my father's side my ancestors were called John. Every male in our family who had ever existed seemed to have been a James or a John. Suddenly I no longer felt unique. It was as if I was carrying on a tradition to keep the name James alive. It was as if my name was more important than me.

One day when I was about five I was playing in the Back with the other children when someone called out "Jim!" from an upstairs window. I naturally turned and looked up, expecting to see Ma's head at our window. She wasn't there. It was someone else who had called out my name, someone else who wanted to tell me something. And then I saw there were five boys of different ages all with their heads cocked, looking around like me and wondering who had called them. They were all called Jim like me! It got worse, for this happened time and time again wherever I went, and I soon realised that half the children in Glasgow were called Jim. And not just the children. There were men being hailed in the street: "Aw right then, Jim?", "How's it going, Jimmy". I was relieved that nobody called me Jimmy as that seemed to be reserved for older men, but my brother would sometimes call me Jimbo, which made me feel like a fat clown. Surely, I deserved better, I thought.

At school, I liked writing my name. I liked to start with an expansive flowing 'J', and I allowed myself a flourish when finishing with the 's'. Writing my signature made me feel good as if it were proof of my existence. But I had to accept that I was just another sheep in the flock with a totally unoriginal name. I even became jealous of my classmates who were called Peter or Stephen and mad at my parents for having no imagination. However, one day Miss Markey, called me to the blackboard, saying in a rather pompous voice, "Come, royal James". I asked her what she meant by "royal", and she told me that the last kings of Scotland had been called James. "Yes," she said, "You have the name of Kings." That cheered me up, and I forgave my parents. I went back to my seat, glancing smugly at the plebeian clods called Peter and Stephen: I was royal!

I also discovered that I had another name. I was called

Fitzpatrick. It was written on a nameplate on our front door. On the neighbour's door there was a brass plate with another name. They were called McFadyen. Everyone behind each door had the same name. So your surname meant you were part of a family. Fitzpatrick also meant something else in Glasgow. It meant I was a Catholic. You couldn't be called Fitzpatrick and be a Protestant. So my name meant that I was part of a family and a religion. I didn't decide this, it was my name which decided who I was and how I would be seen by others. Then I found out that Ma was called Mrs. Fitzpatrick, but that she'd had a different name before she was married to my Da. She had been called Brander. So you could lose your name, if you were a woman. I asked Ma about this once in my usual stumbling way. She replied crossly, "That's just my married name, but I'm *not* a Fitzpatrick!" So who was she then? But I could see she didn't want to go into it. I was puzzled. How can you bear a name and say it's not you, that it's not who you are?

One Hogmanay while we were eating cherry cake, Uncle Jerry told us a funny story about my grandma and her maiden name. He said:

When she went up the aisle to the altar to be married to your grandfather, the priest verified both of their names. So he asked your grandfather to state his name before the congregation and in the sight of God. Your grandfather was a tall fine figure of a man, and he replied proudly "John Fitzpatrick". Then the priest turned to your grandmother, and looking down because she was so tiny, asked her to state her name. And your grandma, who was a shy wee girl, said "Catherine Fitzpatrick." The priest frowned, sighed and then put on a big understanding smile as if he were talking to the village idiot. "No, I mean your maiden name, not the name of your future husband. Now tell us, what's your maiden name?" And your grandma became flustered, defiantly repeating "Catherine Fitzpatrick". There were howls of laughter. Your grandfather was marrying a dimwit, people whispered under their breath. Then your grandma's father stepped forward and pushed the priest in the chest, saying "My name's Fitzpatrick. So, my daughter's called Fitzpatrick. Don't you treat her that way. You're the stupid one, not her!" And the priest reddened, but seeing that he was in the wrong, he proceeded with the ceremony.

Uncle Jerry finished by saying, "So, you've got a double dose of Fitzpatrick blood in you - at least on your father's side."

On the other side was Ma's family: the Branders. I was intrigued by such a strange name. One day I was watching the cowboy series *Rawhide.* A young Clint Eastwood was herding cattle and branding each cow with a burning iron. I asked Ma if that had anything to do with her name. She didn't know, but her sister Peggy said she had heard from their father that they had Protestant ancestors from the North East of Scotland who had once done the same thing as Clint. The only difference was they had branded sheep not cattle. There was a link between Clint and me! It was wonderful. Almost as good as the link with King James. So I found myself in the odd position of being part of two flocks. One was Scottish and Protestant, and the other was Irish and Catholic. But how can you tell if a sheep belongs to one flock or another? Surely, they all look the same. The difference for me, I understood, was that although I had blood links to the Branders I was branded a Fitzpatrick by the State through my father's name, which took precedence over my mother's, and also by the Holy Roman Catholic church through baptism. My school also branded me a Catholic. In Glasgow at that time, strangers could place you by 'innocently' asking which school you attended. When you said "Saint Clare's", they heard the word 'saint', which meant I was a Catholic. Depending on the stranger, he would instantly trust or mistrust you. You were one of his lot - or not.

There were two parts to my name, Fitz and Patrick. A bit like Mac and Douglas or O' and Connell or John and son. Miss Markey explained that these different prefixes and suffixes meant the same thing, and that we were all descended from the sons of distant ancestors. There was a boy called Alec FitzGerald in my class. Miss Markey used me and Alec as examples, saying that 'Fitz' came from the Normans who had come with William the Conqueror in 1066. 'Fitz' came from the French *fils de*, meaning son of. My classmate was descended from his distant ancestor Gerald and I from my distant ancestor Patrick, whom I imagined as a Norman warrior wearing chainmail and carrying a lance as he charged into battle at Hastings. Miss Markey had shown us pictures of the Bayeux Tapestry and had also told us on St Patrick's Day that Patrick had bravely cast out all the venomous snakes from Ireland and had performed all kinds of miracles. My name was really beginning to get interesting: linked to King James, Clint Eastwood, Norman warriors, and now a redoubtable Saint with magic powers! From then on I beamed with pride when my name was called out in class.

But like the priest at my grandma's wedding I soon discovered that there were other families in Easterhouse called Fitzpatrick, and that I didn't just belong to one family, but to a tribe which had all kinds of common ancestors. I realised that there were Fitzpatricks all over the place, at once unconnected (as Da didn't know them), and yet somehow connected through the common name we bore. One day I came into conflict with another Fitzpatrick, an ordeal which left its mark on my childhood memories. I vaguely knew him as we had been at the same primary school.

Going to school at that time was not just about lessons. School was really about playing in the playground at break times and at lunch after we had bolted down our dinner. Then the sad sound of the school bell summoned us back to the serious world of the classroom.

Although girls and boys rarely played with one another in the playground, we were all very conscious of one another, particularly the boys who were always showing off to get the girls' attention. I remember leading my troop of U.S. cavalry men up and down the playground while we trumpeted the theme tune to a John Wayne western, 'She wore a yellow ribbon'. We transformed our snotty handkerchiefs into scarves which we wore over our faces to keep off the desert dust. We trotted around the playground on our way to wage battle against the Mexican army. The girls were not impressed, and nor were a group of boys from another class who jeered: "Stupid little pricks!".

One of these boys was David Fitzpatrick. He was taller than me, and a year older. He was thin, fair-haired and good-looking and he knew that the girls liked him: they would squeal with delight if he caught them when they were playing 'tag'.

Anyway, he came up to us and put his hand out to stop me. Being the cavalry commander, I stopped my horse and eyed the hostile forces. My line of soldiers behind me looked anxiously at the older boys. The girls stopped playing and I heard whispered voices: "the two Fitzpatricks" were about "to have a go at each other". My namesake moved forward and shouldered me out of the way, then he told me to watch where I was going. This made his pals, and some of the girls, snigger to see me put down in such a way. I had no option, being the calvary commander but to reply "Watch it! Just watch where you're going. It's a free country." My last line was one of our favourites. Whenever anyone tried to get us to stop what we were doing, we immediately replied "It's a free country, isn't it?", and carried on. David Fitzpatrick was just about to reply when the bell rang. The girls groaned with disappointment. Things had been about to get exciting. Then my adversary threw out a threat: "I'll see you later, sonny boy" and spat on the ground at my feet. The girls were thrilled and turned to me. "See you then!" I said as defiantly as I could, while shaking inside. The girls shouted gleefully, and ran off to line up and go back into the class-room. "See you" had only one meaning. There was going to be a fight.

The rest of the day was awful. I didn't hear a word the teacher said, and was reprimanded for my "sullen unco-operativeness". Whenever I approached a dreaded event, I would descend into a zombie-like state, while my heart raced. To my classmates I seemed dead calm, but there was a storm raging inside me.

Finally, the bell rang marking the end of lessons, and I had to take up the challenge. Everyone knew what was going to happen. A group of boys and girls had gathered at the far end of the playground, out of sight of the teachers' staffroom. David Fitzpatrick stood grinning in the centre. My pals and the rest of my class followed me to the spot. There was no time for any verbal exchanges. Things had to move fast before an adult got wind of what was happening. All around me I heard my name as if bets were being taken. It was Fitzpatrick this and Fitzpatrick that. But which Fitzpatrick did they mean? Suddenly he jumped on me and knocked me over backwards. Then he started to punch me. I just went wild, and hit back as hard as I could. The girls began screaming. I managed to wrestle myself free of his grip and scrambled to my feet. Then we paced around each other with the large circle of kids crying out for one or other of us to hit his opponent. I don't know how, but I threw myself at him and lashed out with my fists and feet. He seemed surprised, and we both fell over again, and rolled about, tugging at each other's clothes and swiping wildly at one another. Then I heard a loud whistle, and a roared order for all to disperse. I was pulled away by a teacher. The deputy headmistress had David by the collar. I was trembling and speechless. The teachers were yelling at us, but I didn't take in what they were saying. They seemed, however, to be shouting more at my adversary than at me, as being older he was considered to be more responsible for the fight. I only remember the headmaster's final words: "I don't want to hear of this Fitzpatrick versus Fitzpatrick nonsense anymore! All right? It's bad enough the fighting between Rangers and Celtic fans. But two people with the same name. It's insufferable!" Then he pushed us away in opposite directions, telling us to report to his office the following morning at 9 o'clock sharp.

On the way home I was in a state of shock. Hogie was bouncing about in front of me, shouting insults at David Fitzpatrick and his friends, while shadow-boxing and kicking lampposts. Duffy carried my schoolbag, while Mintsy tried to buck me up with praise and encouragement. I realised there was a difference between the mock fighting of my childhood, and the real fighting which I had just experienced. A real fight was like a hallucination as it was over so fast. I was caught up in a vicious world of blows and kicks, surrounded by a chanting hysterical mob. I remembered most of all the adrenalin rush, pushing me on to battle with everything I had, oblivious to the punches. It was only when we were tugged apart by the teachers, giving me time to catch my breath, that I felt terrible pain all over my body. Then I started shaking and tears welled up. I couldn't believe it. I had been in a real fight. And if I hadn't won, neither had I been thrashed or humiliated. A real fight against my namesake, a Fitzpatrick. It troubled me to think that I had fought someone who probably shared some common ancestor. But on seeing that I was coming to my senses, my pals began to joke to lighten the atmosphere. Hogie danced in front of me, punching the air. "So, Fitzpatrick hit Fitzpatrick, but Fitzpatrick retaliated and punched Fitzpatrick who started kicking Fitzpatrick." "But Fitzpatrick won!" Duffy said, lifting up my arm.

And that's all we heard the next day at school. Endless jokes about one Fitzpatrick beating another Fitzpatrick. Everyone suddenly knew my name, and the Fitzpatricks gained a reputation for being fighters, which secretly pleased me to the core. The downside, of course, was my summons to the headmaster's office. I was reprimanded and belted three times, while my opponent received six strokes of the belt. Ma was subsequently summoned to make sure that the battle of the Fitzpatricks would stop there, and not become a war. But Ma didn't mention the incident to Da, and the whole matter died down as quickly as it had flared up.

So I began to feel my name was part of who I was. How can you live without accepting your name, which has been handed down to you from people who lived long before you? I was part of something bigger and older than myself. And yet it made me someone special. It made me feel that I was the standard bearer for my family's name, and that I could put my own stamp upon the name as I went through life, and I could perhaps hand it down to others, who could in turn put their stamp on it.

There were names other than my own, and every other name that I encountered would have a greater or lesser meaning for me. Some names could evoke all kinds of emotions and connections. I only had to hear the names of some of my relations or neighbours or characters from books to instantly conjure up potent images, which seemed as tangible and real as the ground I stood on. The mention of my Auntie Nettie, for instance, took me to a world of comfort, cleanliness and the fragrance of lavender and waxed furniture. There was the delicious sweet smell of buns, fruit cake and hot tea, and the softness of cushions on big cosy armchairs. At the mention of my cousin Lucille, I could see her, and sense her warmth as I sat beside her on the sofa. I could picture her face with its large expressive eyes and radiant smile.

Then there were a host of names like Lancelot, Columbus or Jesse James (another James!) which excited my imagination. And then there were other names which immediately conjured up a fixed image in my mind, names which I had encountered in books or heard about in class or church. When I heard, for instance, John the Baptist's name mentioned by the priest, I would see a poor man clothed in a ragged sheepskin, with dishevelled hair and sunken cheeks, crying in the desert, paving the way for Christ. What a job he had, I thought, having to make 'the crooked roads straight, flatten the mountain tops and fill up every valley'. And all this with his bare hands and with nothing more to eat than locusts. I understood why he was crying his eyes out.

And then there were place names. The more exotic they were, the better. I only had to hear someone mention *Tahiti* and I found myself on a white sandy beach beneath swaying coconut trees, eyes fixed dreamily on the hazy azure sea. I had been born in the Gorbals on the banks of the River Clyde, but now I learned the names of the world's great waterways. I imagined myself on an Egyptian galley floating down the Nile, or navigating the Amazon in my flimsy canoe, surrounded by crocodiles and panthers lazing in the overhanging trees.

One day, Miss Markey explained the difference between a common noun and a proper noun. She said 'a river' was a common noun, and asked if anyone could give her an example of a particular river. With my teeth transformed into crocodile fangs and my eyes blazing like a panther, I raised my hand and said "The Amazon, miss." "Good." she replied, "You see, a proper noun has a particular name. What about another example of a river?" Now I was a Hindu Goddess with eight arms dancing like snakes. "The Ganges, miss", I called out. "Yes, of course," she replied, and added, "And then there's the Clyde, isn't there?"

So even proper nouns could be dull. But for me they were magical. Strange other-worldly names from far away places and times were firing my imagination. And in my mind, I *was* John the Baptist, only I was crying in the wilderness of a 'nameless' council estate, with its mountains of prejudice, valleys of ignorance and its crooked gang-ridden streets.

6. GANGS

My birthplace was universally recognised at that time as the worst place in Glasgow. The Gorbals was on the south side of the Clyde, in other words 'nowhere'. It was a dump. The dark smelly tenement buildings were packed with decent ordinary working-class families like ours, but also with half the alcoholic underclass of Glasgow. The Gorbals was synonymous with gangland for any Glaswegian, and aptly named 'Scar City'. Young hard guys with razors, knives, hammers and broken bottles shared the streets with kids like me. These guys all had scars on their faces.

I have one shattering memory of the Gorbals. When I was four years old I was playing in the street, which was 'safe' as there were no cars, since nobody owned one, when I ran into a lamppost. I was taken to the Royal Infirmary with blood all over my face. We went to the Emergency Department, and waited five hours before being seen, surrounded by battered wives, teenagers with slashed faces and singing drunks. I was given ten stitches at the top of my forehead. The nurse then put a huge bandage all around my head. I felt like one of the Sikhs who worked as ticket collectors on Glasgow's buses. The next day, all the women talked about my stitches. They patted my turbaned head, saying "poor wee thing." Then they spoke about their own teenage boys who had either twenty stitches on their cheeks, or thirty stitches on their neck. I was in my element: four years old with my ten stitches. I was proud. My face was a mess!

Shortly afterwards, I was told that we were leaving the Gorbals - the old worst part of Glasgow, to go to Easterhouse - the new worst part of Glasgow. Half the Gorbals gangsters came along too, so I went from one gangland to another. After we left, the Gorbals was razed to the ground. For once, Glasgow City Council made a good decision. But that was after the bad decision; to build Easterhouse. The difference was that now we had a bath and two real bedrooms and that was certainly an improvement. But we still lived up a tenement surrounded by other tenements inhabited by decent families, but also by people that no other district council wanted to know about. Just the way it had been in the Gorbals. So living conditions were better inside but nothing had fundamentally changed. We continued with the same old problems.

Like all children, I liked my familiar surroundings, but at the same time wanted to broaden my horizons and explore further afield. My home ground was my Close and the neighbouring Closes and streets. Everybody knew each other by sight or reputation. My best pals all lived in the neighbouring streets. I lived in Lochdochart Road, Mintsy in Dunskaith Street, Duffy in one of the select two storey buildings with a garden in Lentram Street, and

Hogie in Denmilne Street. We weren't all living in the same street, but from a very young age we were aware of boundaries. I could safely walk down Dunskaith Street or go up Denmilne Drive, but I knew instinctively that I couldn't go anywhere I wanted. It was an unspoken rule. We were aware and fearful of no-go areas outside of our own domain. "We can't go down there...let's turn back" was a constant refrain. It was strange, we were imprisoned behind invisible bars, created by gangs. They made us believe that we belonged to a territory. That's what the gangs wanted, and that's what they got: ganglands.

There was graffiti everywhere I went. Every tenement wall, every shop shutter, bus shelter and billboard was plastered with gang names. Our district was dominated by four big gangs: The Tongs, the Drummy, the Provvy and the Den-Toi. Every wall had at least one 'TONGS YA BASS!' scrawled on it. The graffiti marked out each gang's territory. Names of other gangs like the BAR-L from Barlanock, meant that they had dared to pass through another gang's territory and leave their mark as provocation. And then there were nicknames of individual gang members scribbled in spray paint: Pinkie...Ness...Kass...and so on. Some of the graffiti was gigantic, covering the whole length and breadth of a wall. Perhaps these guys had big egos: they seemed to be going to great lengths to get noticed. But after a while you didn't see the graffiti anymore. It had become part of the landscape.

My Uncle Jerry often made me think. One Sunday when he dropped by, Ma was complaining about the ugly new graffiti plastered all over our bus shelter, just after it had been freshly painted by the Council. "Look Gena," he said, "These guys don't know what it is to write on paper. They don't know what a pen is, and half of them can't read. All they can do is spray their names on walls. They only know two words: the name of their gang and their own stupid gang name." And he turned to me, as I was hanging about the side of his armchair as I liked to listen to him talk, and smell his after-shave. "And don't you be afraid of them, son. All right? Mind yourself, of course, because some of them are headbangers, but remember that they're the ones who are scared. They're scared of someone like you."

"Me?" I exclaimed, delighted at the idea, but sceptical, "How's that? They're big, and they've got...knives and..."

"Aye," Uncle Jerry continued, "And razors and hammers. I know, but do you know why?"

I shook my head.

"Because they're scared...scared of people like you who can read and write and count. You don't need a hammer or a razor. You've got a brain, son, and they haven't. And do you know who they fight? They fight other brainless wonders like themselves whether it's the Drummy against the Provvy or the Billy Boys against the Cumbie. They're a bunch of morons fighting other morons like themselves."

"But what about the leaders?" I asked, "Aren't they really tough?"

"Aye," he answered, "they're the worst. They manipulate the others and get them to have a square-go with the other gangs". (A 'square-go' was a fight with the same weapons). "These guys are real sadists. They bully weaker ones, generally younger than them, into following them for protection. But they're all cowards at heart like all bullies." He sipped his tea, and finished, saying, "So, don't you worry about them, son. Look, is that not the ice-cream van I can hear outside? Here's two bob - go and get some ginger beer and an ice-cream wafer for you and your brother." That's what I liked about Uncle Jerry. He didn't speak to me as an adult would, but as if he were an older pal giving advice. He also knew that I was a wee boy with a wee boy's taste for sweets and lemonade.

So Uncle Jerry told me not to worry about gangs and I didn't worry so much as I was usually off the streets early in the evening and already in bed when things started. The gangs remained invisible to me, but their graffiti was ever present and so was their reputation. The talk in class was about street battles between gangs and we saw the damage they had left behind when we passed smashed up shops on the way to school. They stayed out of sight like night predators, like foxes. Only occasionally did I see the fox pounce on its prey.

One Saturday afternoon I was playing football with a couple of pals on our favourite 'pitch', the swing-park. Without the numbers to form teams we were just kicking the ball about and trying to score against Stuart, who was in goals. He was three or four years older than us and he outclassed us at football. He stopped all our shots even when we were two yards from the goal. Suddenly he let in a goal - we couldn't believe it! Then we realised that he had made no effort to stop Mintsy's feeble shot as his eyes were elsewhere. "Look," he said. We turned and saw a heavily-built teenager clambering over the railings. He raced past the roundabout and jumped over the railings at the other side of the swing park and bolted off into one of the Closes. And then another teenager leapt over the railings in pursuit. This was Pinkie. He was fair-haired and looked about fifteen. He ran very fast, and he had a knife in his hand. He disappeared into the Close. We turned to Stuart, "Is he going to kill him?" Stuart shrugged his shoulders and said that Pinkie would get the guy either today or on another day. We stared at the Close as if it might be the scene of a bloody murder. So that was Pinkie, I thought. His name was spray-painted all around our area. We had seen the name in person. And the Word became flesh. Pink flesh. Pinkie. So gangs were very real, and I began to wonder if Uncle Jerry was right.

When I was about ten, I became more aware of the 'headbangers'. One of them was a weird guy whom we avoided as much as possible. He was about sixteen and wore a green suit. He was sickly and thin and had a strange way of walking and moving his arms. In fact he never stayed still. He was constantly jerking about, his arms slicing the air with karate blows and his head swivelling as if he expected to be jumped on at any moment. He used to laugh hysterically, showing his rotten teeth, and then became suddenly angry, lashing out with his feet, kicking whatever was near, overturning bins or swiping at any dog that came in sight. He was always accompanied by two or three mean-looking mates, who kept their distance from one another as if wary of their own so-called pal. I didn't understand a word they said. They would shout abuse and burst into laughter that sounded false. They were members of the Drummy. Nobody ever knew the real names of these kinds of guys but their gang names appeared on the surrounding walls alongside dozens of others.

One day I heard that two neighbours were moving house and they were the neighbours I liked the most. Why were they going? I couldn't understand. But around 1965 the atmosphere in the streets had begun to change. There were new families moving into our area and these families were not like us. The men didn't work and the women were very rough-looking, with the downtrodden look of those who have been abused. Their children smelled, and were badly dressed in clothes that were either too small or too big. They didn't wear the school uniform like the rest of us. Three or four came into our class to replace three of the nice girls whose families had left. These newcomers didn't know basic arithmetic and they couldn't read. The teachers didn't know what to do with them. Whenever they were asked a question, they stayed obstinately silent. And during lessons they created problems by fidgeting, pulling the girls' hair, throwing rulers and breaking pencils. They had every chance of ending up in a gang.

Lochdochart Road was one of the main thoroughfares in Easterhouse. It was a busy but safe place. Then all that changed. The gangs decided to use our street as a battleground. In the late evening we would hear shouting in the deserted streets, then the familiar sound of bottles smashing. Suddenly, figures could be seen running down the street, throwing bottles and bricks at their rivals, who scattered and disappeared into the Closes. From time to time, one of the members of a gang would stand in the middle of the street with the full glare of the streetlights upon him, holding up a club or a hammer as if he were a gladiator at the Coliseum. He would scream "Tongs ya bass!" or "Drummy kills!" or simply a string of incomprehensible insults. Then the police sirens could be heard in the distance. They were letting everyone know they were on their way. The gangs vanished in an instant. So when the police arrived with their blue lights flashing there was nothing to see: just the remains of broken bottles and bricks on the road. We were spectators at a show and the final act was always a let-down.

And then something terrible happened to one of my classmates. He wasn't memorable; he was a frail worried-looking boy, quiet and inoffensive. His name was Barry. One day we heard that he had been involved in a gang fight in Drumchapel. His head had been split open by a broken bottle. We never saw him again. I was told he was killed. Others said his family had left to get away from the place. Father Kelly said a mass for him. The whole school was there and we all wondered why his head had been split open. He wasn't a tough guy. He was just like us, innocent, inoffensive and living in a dump which was becoming increasingly violent. Strangely enough, once gone, Barry seemed to exist in a way he never had when he was part of the class.

We could all be beaten up and scarred for life. That's why families were moving away. Nothing was said, but we were uneasy.

Then Frankie Vaughan came to Easterhouse accompanied by the national press, and we thought we had been saved. He was one of the '60's 'crooners' who lingered on after the Beatles revolution, but he still warmed the hearts and minds of older generations. He was good-looking and had starred in a film with Marilyn Monroe. For some reason he began a crusade against delinquency in Easterhouse. He sought to use his 'suave voice to soften the hardened hearts of the gang members'. That was what we read in the papers. Now Easterhouse was on the map and it was unanimously voted the worst place to live in Britain. Thank you, Frankie.

But our great crooner did manage, nevertheless, to persuade the gang leaders to come together and sign a kind of peace treaty. He also raised funds to build a community centre for young people. It was made of corrugated iron and looked like a Nissen Hut. There was plastic furniture and two table tennis tables inside. The gangs were supposed to go there and live in harmony, playing table tennis while listening to the sultry songs of Frankie.

It didn't actually work out that way. The national press soon got bored with the inarticulate louts and left. The peace treaty soon fell apart and the community centre, which had rapidly become covered in gang graffiti, was trashed and the table tennis tables smashed. That seemed to be the end of any hope for Easterhouse. The place simply went downhill, and the gangs got worse. My pal Duffy left, as his parents couldn't stand it any longer, and his father's car had been smashed up several times.

Even worse for me was the tragic news that the parents of Ann Bolan, the most beautiful girl in the class, had decided to move as well. What was the point in going to school now? Beauty had deserted the classroom. I was sick at heart. Everyone was leaving, to be replaced by the social misfits, the unemployed and the wife-beaters. The gangs had got what they wanted: territories full of graffiti-splashed walls, closed and boarded-up shops, smashed-up bus shelters and a whole new generation of semi-literate kids brought up by alcoholic parents.

'Tongs ya bass!' seemed to shout at us from every wall. They were calling us bastards, but they were the bastards. They contributed to two depressing statistics which went against the demographic trends in Britain at that time. The population of Easterhouse fell from over 56 thousand in the mid 1960's to just over eight thousand today. And Easterhouse had the lowest number of foreign-born inhabitants in the U.K. In other words, even the poorest of immigrants avoided the place. It seemed to me that there was only one thing to do - leave. And I did, but I had to wait until I was 18.

7. THE POOL

At first there were many things I didn't like about swimming pools, and the main one was swimming itself. Maybe that was because I taught myself the hard way. It all began when my friends and I heard about a swimming pool in Coatbridge, a former mining town a couple of train stops away from Easterhouse. It had never occurred to the Council to build a swimming pool for us, and none of us could swim. But we all decided to learn. Ma grudgingly agreed to buy me a pair of swimming trunks. They were bright blue and three sizes too big. When I put them on I felt like one of the Three Musketeers in my big breeches. She said I would grow into them; in about ten years, I thought.

Entering the dressing rooms at the swimming pool was like going into a chemical factory. The smell of chlorine was overpowering. Getting undressed was a tricky business because although we presented a tough, confident exterior, we had been brought up to be rather prim and prudish about nudity. So, I quickly took off my underpants and, blushing furiously, hurriedly pulled on my baggy trunks. We were like the slogan for the Omo soap powder advert: 'Whiter than white'. Brought up in sunless Glasgow, the whiteness of our skin was only broken by the blue of our veins. Mintsy was incredibly skinny and we poked fun at him as we could see his rib-cage. He was as translucent as a boiled sweet, and he truly lived up to his nickname. Duffy was the only one who looked decent as he was well built and had a good pair of trunks that actually fitted him.

Going into the water was an awful experience. It was like a bath of cold bleach. Our eyes turned flaming red and our nostrils burned and we started coughing like asthmatics. At first, we held on nervously to the side of the pool at the shallow end, standing on tip-toe with our heads cocked up to breathe. The bigger boys jumped in and pushed each other around, creating choppy waves which splashed our faces. The noise was deafening. Everyone was yelling their heads off. I was embarrassed when my oversized trunks blew up like balloons. Little by little, however, we stopped clinging to the side and began to bounce up and down and giggle nervously as we slapped water at each other.

We built up enough confidence to try jumping into the shallow end. Scared out of my wits, I took the plunge and parachuted into the water, my trunks billowing out beneath me. My pals followed suit. At last we were beginning to enjoy ourselves. Then a whistle blew, and everyone wearing yellow armbands was told to get out by an old guy in a white tracksuit who was supposed to be the lifeguard. He didn't look as if he could get his his shoes off fast enough to save anyone from drowning. We'd been given yellow bands at the entrance. "But, we've just arrived!" we complained. The old geezer ordered us out of the pool, saying our time was up and rules were rules. Swimming sessions, we discovered, lasted forty-five minutes and no more. Reluctantly, we clambered out, but then jumped back in which maddened the old man. He threatened to ban us for good if we didn't come out at once. We glumly obeyed, and came out agreeing that we should get undressed much faster next time.

Outside the swimming pool, shivering and holding our wet towels, we discovered something which encouraged us to return the following week. It was an ice-cream café run by an Italian, predictably called Tony, like so many Glaswegian Italians. Tony had every flavour imaginable: mint, strawberry, chocolate, lemon - whatever you wanted. The ice cream van that did the rounds of Easterhouse only had boring vanilla. Duffy was the only one with spare cash so we complimented him on his stylish trunks and the fearless way he jumped into the water. Then we told him what flavour we wanted. Flattered, Duffy forked out like the good pal he was.

I took a book out of the library on how to swim, and I studied it obsessively after school. I lay face down on my bed with the book open on the pillow and tried to copy the breast stroke movements in the series of illustrations. It seemed so easy. I felt confident. But at the swimming pool the following week it was another story. On pushing off I found myself huffing, puffing and gasping for breath while I flapped about. My unsynchronised limbs were going in all directions. With my head craned upwards to avoid the chlorine, I moved my arms in and out as rapidly as I could while my legs dangled and jerked about behind me. Finally my efforts were repaid, and I managed to move a few feet forward without touching the bottom. I was over the moon - I could swim!

After a few sessions I managed to achieve my first goal of swimming from one side of the pool to the other. We spurred each other on and soon there was no stopping us. We were little frogs swimming breadth after breadth. But we were still at the shallow end where we could always stand after bumping into someone or swallowing some water. The real challenge was the deep end. There was a different atmosphere there. Compared to the noisy turbulence of the shallow end, the deep end was almost calm - at least before we arrived. There was a scary colder feeling about the water as we gripped the side and felt our feet dangling beneath us. Here were people who could swim like the woman in my book. These people glided effortlessly through the water. We still had a lot to learn. Undeterred, we undertook to swim a breadth across the deep end, which seemed as wide as the Channel. Giggling nervously to hide our terror, we launched into the deep. I thrashed my arms around like a windmill, horrified by the emptiness beneath me. Duffy got to the other side first, then Hogie, and even Mintsy before I finally spluttered up to join them. We congratulated ourselves on accomplishing such a great feat and then set off again, and again until we were no longer intimidated by the deep. From that moment, the pool was ours.

The following Saturday we transformed the swimming pool into the 'jumping pool'. Now that we felt we could go into the deep end and swim back to the side, we turned our attention to jumping into the water in the most elaborate or ridiculous way. The first few tentative jumps were a test of our nerves. We trembled at the side, urging one another to jump. Hogie was the first to go in. He was a great guinea pig as he had no fear, and lacked the imagination to anticipate the worst. Then I leapt in with a terrific splash and sank into the deep with my trunks puffed up. Desperately holding my breath, I finally emerged, spluttering but proud, to finish with a clumsy doggie paddle to the side. Soon we were trying to out-jump each other. Then, when the old lifeguard wasn't looking, we took running jumps and leapt clutching our knees like depth-charges. This created the biggest splashes, but also the biggest headaches when you hit the water face first. We did daring jumps, performing twirls and scissor kicks, and kicking imaginary balls. We were cartoon characters, suspended in mid-air for an instant before plunging down. Jumping in again and again meant clambering out again and again. It was exhausting, so we were relieved to hear the end of session whistle.

Our next challenge was the two diving boards: one a low spring-board and the other a diving dale about eight metres high. We started on the springboard. We were pirates being made to walk the plank above a shark-infested sea. We bounced up and down with wobbly legs and were catapulted into the deep end. We were human canon balls, circus performers, rocket men blasted into the pool. Duffy could bounce higher than the rest of us, spring up and finish with a 'depth-charge', and a tremendous splash.

Next was the really big ordeal: the high diving dale. We climbed up, pretending to be shivering with the cold, but actually trembling with fear. When we looked down from the top we were shocked: it seemed the diving dale had increased its height four-fold. We had lots of experience of jumping down stairs or off walls but nothing had prepared us for this. We were about to chicken out and go back down when, to our dismay, a wee girl of about six came up with her big brother and both of them dived together into the pool. We couldn't believe it. We looked down and saw the girl pop her head out of the water and swim gracefully to the side, quite nonchalantly. We looked at each other. We were not to be out-done.

We picked Hogie to go first. He protested but we egged him on, and eventually he went to the edge. He didn't hesitate but simply jumped and miraculously survived. We saw him doing a side-stroke back to the edge of the pool with his fist raised triumphantly. Mintsy was shaking and on the verge of tears, so we didn't insist that he jump. So Duffy went next, saying "See you in Heaven...". He dropped straight as a die and popped into the water as if he had done it a dozen times before. I knew that if I jumped I would make a mess of it - and I did. I threw myself off the dale and smashed into the water with a perfectly angled belly-flop. The pain was excruciating. I felt as if I had been whacked in the stomach with a plank of wood. When I managed to struggle out of the pool, spewing water, my skin was bright red. On seeing this, Mintsy sheepishly backed down the stairs. We didn't jeer at him as we would normally have done. In fact, this made us feel more heroic. Two Saturdays later, Mintsy gathered up the courage to drop off the dale. He was proud, and a worthy member of our gang once more. We sportingly applauded his bravery.

But the 1964 Olympics in Tokyo put a stop to our jumping antics. Watching the games on TV, I was amazed by the perfection and speed of the athletes. We could only do a laboured kind of breaststroke and doggie-paddle. In Tokyo we saw what swimming really could be, especially when we saw Don Schollander, the Tarzan-esque four-time gold medal winner. And then there were the spectacular diving events. We gasped at the triple somersaults, back-flips and jack-knifes before the athletes slid into the water without a ripple. We were inspired by our Olympic champions. No more jumping or kids' stuff. Swimming had become a serious business.

We practised our strokes on the way to school. We swung our arms backwards and forwards and twisted our heads right and left as we powered along the pavement doing the crawl. We tried the butterfly but soon gave up, realising that you had to be a Don Schollander to perform that stroke. We did a slow rhythmic breast-stroke, breathing like professionals. We must have looked ridiculous.

Back at the pool we tried to improve our strokes. Doing breaststroke, I could never quite coordinate the movements. I was more successful at the crawl, but I was still pretty awful. Then I discovered a stroke which suited me better than the others. It was the backstroke. Here I could swim and breathe at the same time. It was a Godsend!

The only problem was that I couldn't see where I was going, which meant regular collisions.

We had races which Duffy always won hands down. He even managed to master turning over at the end of each length and kicking off which none of the rest of us ever achieved.

But swimming was just too exhausting so I decided to become an Olympic diver. I took a book out of the library which showed all the movements for each dive. The photos showed a man who was always perfectly straight or at a 90° angle or perfectly curled into a ball. My favourite was the jack-knife: you sprang off the diving board, touched your toes, then plunged straight into the water. I began practising toe-touching in my bedroom. My face was red and my knees shook but I could never touch my toes for long. So I decided to create my own special version of the jack-knife.

I wanted to impress my pals with my sophisticated dives. But I only performed them once, for obvious reasons. Take my back-flip dive when I missed the side of the pool by a fraction of an inch. Or one dreadful plunge from the dale when my dive turned into a belly-flop. I felt like I had slapped onto a concrete slab. My pals jumped in to pull me out as they could see I was dazed and barely able to stay afloat. The time had come for me to reconsider my Olympic diving aspirations.

But first, I had to give myself one last chance to showcase my dramatic creation, the 'shin' jack-knife. But I could see from my pals' polite applause that my valiant effort was pretty underwhelming. It was time to stop showing off. Firstly, I had nothing to show off, and secondly, I didn't actually like diving that much.

Then one day something wonderful happened. I had intended to do a simple dive from the side of the pool but this time I glided perfectly into the water. Not only that, but I was carried along and found myself at the other side of the pool. I felt brilliant. I was not even out of breath. I was a giant manta ray gliding through the sea. I realised I had my eyes open and I could see all around: the dangling legs of children, swimmers moving above. I could swim underwater! There was something thrilling about gliding, weightless and at one with the elements. Sometimes I was a dolphin, sometimes I moved like a giant turtle, but mostly I was a white shark nosing about in the deep.

I had discovered an environment that I could really enjoy. I realised that I shouldn't be too hard on myself. I was never going to be a great Olympic diver, but it didn't matter. I had found pleasure. The happy little frog had become a Prince - a Prince of the Deep!

8. CHURCH

I was loved by God. That's what the priest told me and that made me feel good. At least somebody loved me. God seemed pretty nice. But then I was introduced to the Bible in Religious Instruction lessons, and I discovered that He had another side. God, in fact, could be pretty mean. Striking down the Pharaoh and the Egyptians with plagues of locusts, turning Lot's wife into a pillar of salt, raining down fire and brimstone on Sodom and Gomorrah and causing rain for forty days and nights, which was even worse than in Glasgow. And those were just the opening pages. The Bible, in fact, was a good read. It made a great change from the soppy *Janet and John* books which we had been given to teach us how to read and write. I loved the stories of David outsmarting Goliath; Samson and the treacherous Delilah; and poor old Job and his lousy family, who abandoned him as he fell from riches to rags.

Then there was Jesus. His miracles really impressed me. Bringing Lazarus back to life, healing the blind and the lame, feeding the multitude with only five loaves and two fishes, and even walking on water. What I couldn't understand was why he let himself be lashed, crowned

with thorns and crucified. Why on earth didn't he perform a miracle, bring forth thunderbolts from the Heavens and annihilate the tormenting Romans and Philis-
tines? He helped everyone else, so why not himself? I kept
my bewilderment to myself, put my palms together and
prayed, as I had been instructed to do by Father Kelly and
Father Docherty. But nothing happened when I got down
on my knees. Nothing I ever prayed for came to pass. And
everything I prayed to stop happening, just kept on happening. Obviously I hadn't got the hang of it yet.

I really had no luck. My mother was a Protestant who,
on marrying my Catholic father, took a vow to allow their
children to be brought up Catholic. So I was baptised a
Catholic. That meant observing the sacraments, praying,
denying myself at Lent and, worst of all, having to go
to mass every Sunday morning when all the Protestant
boys I played football with were still tucked up snugly in
bed. I hated mass. We went to St. Clare's church, a pre-
fabricated concrete-slab monstrosity, perfectly in keeping with the rest of the council estate. I felt like I was
walking into a prison. The unaccompanied children of
my age were rounded up at the entrance by an ugly, bony-
faced man with a permanent scowl and a huge Adam's
apple. It disgusted us when he spoke: it looked like he was
trying to swallow a mouse. He pushed us up the aisle to
the front rows so that he could keep an eye on us. He
flapped his arms about when we had to sing hymns or re-
spond to the priest's chanting. We bowed our heads and
mumbled in that incomprehensible and solemn way that
adults do. Mass was tedious. Just like school. It seemed to

me that whenever adults were in charge everything was dead boring.

One of the great inventions of the Catholic church is Confession. You go along, burdened by sin, and come out of the cubicle pure, cleansed, and ready to sin all over again. Protestants, I had to admit, didn't have that privilege. Their sins stuck to their souls, which got darker and more disfigured with the years. I imagined the soul as a big marrow bone like the ones at the butchers. It was inside you, the tarnished mirror of your actions. Waiting to go into Confession was traumatic as I tried desperately to think of all the sinful acts I had committed during the week. Eating my brother's toast behind his back? Was that a sin? I wanted to impress Father Kelly, and grumpy old Father Docherty, with a long list, but that was difficult. I didn't steal or cheat at school or miss mass or 'covet my neighbour's wife', whatever that meant. What was left? So I mumbled out a list as if I were reciting my times tables: "Forgive me father for I have sinned. I disobeyed my parents three times, lied four times, ate too much five times, didn't wash the back of my neck six times..." and so on until I was stopped by the priest who told me to recite ten Hail Marys. I rattled off the prayers at the speed of light. I left the church, beaming with my sense of renewed spiritual spotlessness. Now I could gobble a packet of biscuits as soon as I got home. I was starting my sin-list afresh.

One year, however, I became obsessed by religion and convinced myself that I had to lead the life of a saint. That was at the time of my first communion and confirmation. I had just been told about Saul's conversion on the Road to Damascus. God shone his light upon him and he became Saint Paul. That was what I wanted. I lifted my eyes to the Heavens on the road to school, hoping that I would hear a voice and a light would shine through the black clouds scudding over Glasgow. Nothing happened. But I believed that God was somehow still watching over me behind the heavy grey mantle of cloud. One day, my time would come.

My first Holy communion finally arrived. We had been practising for weeks, going up and down the aisle and kneeling at the altar rail. To prepare me, my Auntie Kathleen, who was a devout believer, had given me a white prayer book with a sweet Virgin Mary on the cover. She said that the Virgin Mary was the Mother of Christ and that if I prayed to her She would intercede on my behalf to her son, Jesus in Heaven. That's what I needed to make my prayers work, I thought, as I thanked her for the gift. Some help at last!

Wearing our new clothes, my class lined up to walk up the aisle as we had practiced. Soon it was my turn to kneel at the altar rail. Father Kelly approached and I opened my mouth as wide as possible as if I was at the dentist, and stuck out my tongue as our teacher had ordered. I was excited. God was about to be put onto my tongue. One swallow and God would be in my belly, lifting up my soul. The priest said "Corpus Christi" and placed the wafer-thin host on my tongue. I gulped, but God wouldn't go down; the wafer was stuck. I wanted to stick my finger in my mouth and move the host, but our teacher had warned us, on pain of going to Hell, never to touch the Body of Christ. So I walked back down the aisle, squirming and sucking. Auntie Kathleen frowned as I passed, with my tongue sticking out and my eyes watering. Thank God, He finally broke into pieces and slipped down. I was glad to have the Body of Christ within me at last. And to my great relief, the priest was the only one allowed to drink his blood. Dracula films had put me right off that part of communion.

The sacrament of Confirmation was better. I was lucky that day, as on the previous night I had jammed my thumb in the kitchen table drawer and cut my hand with a knife. I had a huge bandage around my thumb and wrist. It looked as if I had been bitten by a wolf. My pals were all jealous. I walked proudly up the aisle, wearing a red sash across my chest, this time to take up arms and be confirmed as a soldier of God, and fight His enemies which, to my delight, the priest said were numerous. I imagined that from then on I would spend my life slaying dragons like St Michael. I also liked the idea of being called a 'Roman' Catholic. I imagined myself as a Roman centurion in armour with a feathered helmet, leading forth my legionaries to annihilate the heretics and sinners. My first assault would be on the Brig Bar where Da got drunk with his mates on Fridays and Saturdays.

That year, Lent was a must. Obsessed by outdoing one another, my pals and I set ourselves what we thought were tremendous challenges. I would not read comics for six weeks nor eat chocolate biscuits, although I reserved the right to eat plain ones. We encouraged Duffy to walk barefoot to school, but his mum stopped him, and belted him round the ears. We regarded him as a martyr. Mintsy decided to take a vow of silence for six weeks. But our teacher wasn't amused when he stared back mutely, refusing to answer questions. Three strokes of the belt soon broke his vow. Dissatisfied with my sacrifices, great though I regarded them, I swore to attend mass every morning before school at the neighbouring St Benedict's. Our teacher had set out this possibility, and four of us promised to attend. I can't hide the fact that my choice was influenced when Ann Bolan volunteered to be part of the group. Ann Bolan was the class beauty. She had an angelic face with glowing pink cheeks, just like the image of the Virgin Mary on my prayer book. Her dad was a police sergeant. He must have told her to have nothing to do with toe-rags like us, as she never looked our way. I would have done anything for her, but she never noticed me, even when I did extraordinary things in the playground like scoring incredible goals, or throwing Duffy's bag over the school fence. But now, I thought, she would be bound to see me or even speak to me, if she saw me at mass every day. Every morning I set off for the eight o'clock mass with a hole in my stomach, having skipped my Sugar Smacks. The mass was thankfully a short one with no sermons or long readings. Unfortunately, the priest separated the boys from the girls so I couldn't sit beside or behind Ann and gaze dreamily at her hair and neck. And she didn't speak to me, but only talked to her plain classmate, Shona McKinnon. Coming back to class, however, was magic. Since St Benedict's was quite a distance from the school, we had permission to arrive after class had started. We came in with halos over our heads and took our places with saintly expressions. Not having break-fasted, we were allowed to eat as long as we did it "unostentatiously", as the teacher advised. Nothing could have been more ostentatious than our efforts. Everyone's eyes were glued enviously on us, as we chomped our jam sandwiches and gazed beatifically around.

But my Holy spell didn't last very long after Lent. Having been to enough masses to last a lifetime, I went back to my comics and chocolate biscuits. What troubled me most about God was that He was 'everywhere' and that He was 'infinite'. I just couldn't grasp the meaning of infinity. The priests used the word continually to describe God, but my mind boggled at the idea.

So, what on earth was infinity? I learned multiplication tables quite easily. On the way to school we used to snap out 9 times 6, 8 times 12, and we had to answer in a split second. Then we started with the 13 times and 14 times. We played with decimals, and our heads would swim with 10,000 times 100,000. Then from millions we went to billions and trillions. You could always count more and reach staggering sums. There was always a larger number. Was this what the priests meant by infinity? I began to regard them as sloppy thinkers, and take them less seriously, except for Father Kelly (because he frightened us).

Occasionally Father Kelly would come to our house and stay for as long as it took for Ma to make a pot of tea and for him to gulp down a quick cup. He had a red nose and carnation cheeks, which I put down to all the blood of

Christ that he drank. He didn't speak to my Ma, a Protestant, or to us, but only to Da. I soon realised that he was just like the insurance man who came once a week to collect his payment, or the Mafia in the movies, extorting money from the neighbourhood. He gave Da a packet of blue envelopes, and made him swear on his rosary that he would faithfully fill them with shillings, not pennies, and put them in the collection plate every Sunday. It seemed to me that Father Kelly was offering another form of insurance, or worse, threatening to send us to Hell if we didn't pay up. It annoyed me that he didn't look at me or give me a medal. Me! A soldier of God who went without chocolate biscuits and comics, and went to mass every day for six bleeding weeks on the trot. What more did he want? The first cracks in my faith began to appear.

But then the Lord sent a sign and my faith was restored. Charlton Heston played Moses in *The Ten Commandments.* He was magnificent: tall, tanned, strong and handsome. His chest filled the screen. His eyes blazed with the light of God. Why weren't the men in our congregation like Charlton Heston? They were old, withered, and spineless with pale sunken faces, pot bellies and eyes like toads. I puffed out my chest and opened my eyes wide and tried to speak from the depths of my shoes in a deep booming voice. The Spirit of God, helped by Hollywood, was within me again. Like Moses I wanted to lead my people. I would lead them from the slums of Easterhouse to 'The Promised Land'. I couldn't get him out of my mind. At the swimming pool I stood on the diving board, and opened my arms to part the waters of the Red Sea. But the only parting of waters was when Hogie dive-bombed below me. Undaunted, I knew that when God was behind you, you could do powerful things. I wanted to be a saint or a prophet. Then I would have God's backing to do wonderful things; for me, for the world, and also for Ann Bolan.

As the school Nativity play approached I could see myself playing one of the Three Wise Men bearing gifts to the Mother of God. I wanted to be one of them because Ann Bolan had been chosen to play Mary. Not knowing what frankincense or myrrh actually were, I wanted to lay pots of gold at her feet, look up into her eyes and be noticed at last. But Miss Markey decided otherwise. I was to play Herod! That would make it very difficult for Ann to like me, I lamented. How can you like someone who wants to slay your new-born baby? I begged Miss Markey to let me play Joseph, so that I could be Ann's loving husband. Or even, if it came down to it, a shepherd boy worshipping Jesus (and His mother). I would even play the ox or the ass if I could be beside Mary. But no, she insisted that I was a born Herod. So I was dressed in a red nightgown, a blue party hat that was supposed to be vaguely Arabian, and boot polish was applied to my chin to give me a black beard. I tried to impress Ann by making a point during my speech to the Three Wise Men. I told them to find Jesus, but that they mustn't harm His mother. They should treat her kindly and honourably. And when I ordered the slaughter of all children under two, I ordered my soldiers to comfort the mothers, particularly those called Mary.

When I next went to confession I asked Father Kelly

to forgive me for playing the part of Herod, and I swore that I didn't wish to kill poor baby Jesus, and that I really worshipped him, and his mum. Father Kelly forgave me… and told me again to say ten Hail Marys. I started off in my usual way like an excited football commentator, but then I stopped at one of the lines: "Blessed art thou amongst women…" And I thought of Ann Bolan. I saw her eyes, her cheeks, her lips, her hair…and I kept repeating "Blessed art thou amongst women." I was on my knees at her feet. I was looking up at her. She was putting her hand on my shoulder. But it was only Father Kelly towering above me, and gripping me as if he wanted to crush me. But at last I had something to confess: evil thoughts in the House of God. Father Kelly told me to kneel down again, and recite twenty Our Fathers in his presence. I humbly complied.

Unfortunately for God, I saw another Charlton Heston film which was even better than *The Ten Commandments,* and made me forget Moses. It was *Ben Hur.* Going up mountains and bringing down stone tablets was alright, but nothing could compare with the excitement and thrills of a chariot race. Watching Ben Hur careering round the Coliseum in a chariot pulled by white horses showed me what I wanted from life. He was the glorious underdog, the righteous rebel, the strong and noble hero. That's how I imagined I would be in the future. I would work on my biceps, get a tan, (which would mean leaving Glasgow), and do stretching exercises, get taller and be like Ben Hur. Maybe then, Ann Bolan would sit up and take notice.

Time went by, but for all my efforts my biceps remained

puny and my skin as pale as a sheet under the Glasgow clouds. I began to have real doubts. Then one Sunday, my father wasn't around for some reason. Although he never accompanied me to mass and only went to mass himself about once a month, he always insisted that I had to attend. It was lashing with rain and Ma was indulging in a lie in, glad to be rid of my father for a while. A little devil climbed onto my shoulder and convinced me to play ill. I acted it out well, groaning in sorrow that I would have to skip mass. The following Sunday I was struck with the same mysterious illness, and skipped mass again. Now I had two real mortal sins to confess to Father Kelly, but it disturbed me to think that I didn't really care whether I had committed a mortal sin or not. I continued to go to mass on and off, but with every absence it became harder to return. I didn't understand what was happening to me. I felt that there was a terrible emptiness in church and that the mass was a meaningless ritual.

One day when I was about twelve, I noticed that my brother had left a few books in our room. One of the titles caught my eye; *The Rebel,* by Albert Camus. I flicked through it, but it was incomprehensible to my young mind. Nevertheless, there was something which made an impact. Something about the 'absurd'. Was everything basically absurd? Did the universe itself have no meaning? If so, then Father Kelly's preaching was absurd as well. Everything began to drop into place. That's why I was bothered by the infinite. That's why there was a silence when I tried to pray. That's why there was evil and injustice. It wasn't because of the Devil. It was absurd to think that he existed. It was all man's fault. It was for men to create meaning in their existence, either to fall into drunkenness like Da or to be like Ben Hur, fighting tyranny and injustice. I decided to be a rebel; the only option in an absurd universe.

The following Sunday I went to mass for the last time. I arrived late, and sat in the back row, more or less out of sight. I watched the proceedings, feeling detached, and didn't even pretend to genuflect or bow my head. I felt I was watching a pantomime. The altar boy tinkled the bell to signal the end of the mass. The priest turned to face the congregation, saying: "May the Lord be with you." I turned my back and walked out, without the Lord.

I walked across the windswept football pitches behind the church, feeling as if I had just started out on a long walk to an unknown destination. But I didn't feel troubled, I felt exhilarated. For the first time in my life I felt free to reject what I thought was wrong, and free to choose what I would believe in, as the future unfolded. I raised my fist to the heavens above. I hadn't become a saint, but I had become unshackled. My conversion was as dramatic as Saul's.

9. COMICS

On Saturdays I got my pocket money, and I would go to the paper shop and gaze with wonder at the big jars of brightly coloured sweets on the shelves. There were all sorts: yellow sherbet-lemons with fizzy white centres, gooseberry-shaped *soor plooms*, which you could suck for hours before they dissolved on your green tongue, gooey toffee butternuts which stuck your teeth together, or the cheapest of them all, cardboard-tasting rice pop corns. When I had chosen my threepence worth of Liquorice All Sorts or maybe some creamy caramels, the shop assistant would reach up for one of the big jars, twist open the lid and pour the sweets into a small paper bag, handing it to me with all the solemnity of a priest administering Holy Communion.

The paper shop was narrow, with two counters, squeezed between the Co-op and Galbraiths where Ma did her weekly shopping. On Sundays I loved to go there before mass to get milk and freshly baked rolls knowing that I would enjoy a big breakfast when I came back from communion.

But on Wednesdays I walked straight past the sweets and queued at the newspaper counter to make my precious purchase. Wednesday was the day when the first of my favourite weekly comics was on sale. Wednesday was Beano day! There was a huge pile of them beside the dull mountains of black and white newspapers. My Beano was like a rainbow alongside them: it was bright red and green and yellow. There was nothing like the first touch of the crisp new paper, and the first sight of this week's edition with all my favourite characters. The star was unquestionably Dennis the Menace with his tousled shock of black hair, his scowling face and his famous red and black hooped jumper. He was forever up to tricks: tying tin cans to cats' tails, leaving banana skins at the foot of stairs, putting buckets of water on top of doors which had been left ajar, or firing his catapult which inevitably broke his neighbours' windows. He was a real terror. And at the end of his mischief-making, there was a final cartoon showing his father holding up a huge leather slipper, about to spank him.

Then there were the other characters: Roger the Dodger, Minnie the Minx, and the Bash Street Kids. They were all scruffy, hopeless at school and always up to no good. Reading the Beano was like coming out of confession - Dennis the Menace and all the other pranksters made me feel like an angel. Maybe that's why I loved my comic. It plunged me into a world where children were forever breaking the rules. It was exciting to see what I wasn't supposed to do. It was easy to be a good wee boy when you could read about the roguish high jinks of the Beano's lawless characters.

The Beano's rival comic, the Dandy, had one character

who really captured my imagination. Desperate Dan was a huge cowboy with a massive jaw covered in prickly black stubble. He ate gigantic cow pies with horns sticking out of them like candles on a birthday cake, which gave him tremendous strength. It was said that Desperate Dan had the strength of a hundred men, but the brain of less than one. That's why I liked his stories. He was dim and awkward, but he always fought his way out of his predicaments, and finished by tucking into a gigantic pie, a big smile on his grizzly face.

In Da's newspaper there was always a cartoon at the back. The ones I liked most were Oor Wullie and The Broons which appeared in the Sunday Post. These were short strip cartoons published every week, but then a whole collection of new stories appeared in an annual which made a fantastic Christmas present. Christmas just wouldn't have been the same without them. I treasured them, and turned to them when I was bored with other presents. I would snuggle up in my bed, and take my time to read them, relishing the wonderful feeling that there were many more episodes to come, not just the one short strip that we were offered on Sunday mornings.

Somehow, Oor Wullie always seemed to be the same age as me. He was a small wiry boy with spiky fair hair and a screwed-up face. He always wore the same white shirt and black dungarees, and he spent his time outdoors with his pals, Fat Boab and Soapy Soutar. At the beginning and at the end of his adventures, he would sit on an upturned bucket, hands on his cheeks and elbows on his knees. At the beginning of each episode he would think up a new money-making scheme or some prank. Then after a comic adventure, he would reflect on what he had done. The idea of sitting and thinking before and after you act made a big impression on me.

In some scenes Wullie's mother would make him howl as she scrubbed his ears with a scrubbing brush, or his father would appear at the wrong moment and catch him up to no good. But they were background figures who simply got in the way of Wullie's fun. The only thing that mattered was his life outdoors with his pals and that's why I could identify with him. I felt that I only really existed outside of my home and out of my parents' sight. And yet there was the comforting 'Oor' in Oor Wullie, which showed that he belonged to a family. My ma referred to me as 'Oor Jim' to the neighbours, and they spoke about 'Oor Hughie' or 'Oor Betty'. 'Oor' made you part of a family. Wullie's get-rich-quick schemes usually ended in calamity, and he would cry 'Crivvens!' 'Jings!' and 'Help, ma Boab!' when ticked off by P.C. Murdoch. Other comic characters would exclaim 'Gosh!' 'Oww!', 'Yaargh!' Nobody said 'sorry' or 'thank you' in comics. It was a world of extreme reactions: angry shouts, lamentations, triumphant shrieking. My pals and I copied our favourite characters' wild exclamations. We thought it was our secret language which our parents didn't understand, and that it helped to keep them out of our world.

The Broons were different from other cartoon characters. They were a 'realistic' Scottish family who lived up a Close like us, but a Close which looked more like our old blackened tenement building in the Gorbals. Paw

Broon sported a walrus moustache, Maw Broon was tall and matronly, and Granpaw had a white beard. They had eight kids, ranging from grown up Daphne and Joe, to the young twins and 'The Bairn'. A drama would unfold and they would go from one crisis to another. There was something familiar about them, which was reassuring. They were ordinary people coping with all the little snags and pickles in life. I devoured these stories, my eyes darting from one frame to the next, at once forgetting the story I'd read just minutes earlier.

The Broons, Oor Wullie and the Beano characters were the constant companions of my early childhood. I read the cartoon strips but I didn't laugh, despite the hundreds of jokes and ludicrous situations, because their lives seemed to mirror my own.

But in time Desperate Dan's upper-cuts, and Dennis the Menace's chortle as he put a stink bomb in a bowl of flowers all began to feel silly and childish. I needed new stimulus, and thankfully it wasn't hard to find. In the paper shop I discovered a pile of comics I hadn't noticed before: 'Action Comics'.

The gargoyle-featured Bash Street kids and green-eyed Korky the Cat were now replaced by life-like images of grim-faced, steely-eyed soldiers, heroic adventurers and tenacious sportsmen. I began to read the Hotspur, Valiant, and Victor and many more. In each there was a two or three page story set in the Second World War. The front covers of the Victor and Valiant showed action-packed battle scenes of British soldiers storming Nazi strongholds or Marines battling against the Japanese on beaches and in jungles. I read so much about armies that I could identify any soldier by their uniform and helmet. I learned how to throw a grenade, launch a mortar, use a flame-thrower, attack with a bayoneted rifle, throw sticks of dynamite, position a bazooka on my shoulder, and steer a tank at night. All essential stuff for a boy of my age.

Then there were stories about football and rugby teams, athletes and yachtsmen. There was Roy of the Rovers, the dogged sporting captain of the Rovers football team, eternal underdogs, who somehow always managed to score a cracking winner in the last minute of extra time. And there was Alf Tupper, the 'Tough of the Track', battling against the odds to cross the finishing line.

There were Wild West stories too, like 'The Taming of Sitting Bull'. I loved the drawings of wild-eyed horses bucking and galloping over the plains. There were also spy stories like 'The Wolf of Kabul'. Mysterious men in trench coats would try to destroy the planet. Fortunately, Britain had many clever, plucky heroes who confounded their diabolical plots week after week.

The problem for my mates and me was the sheer number of these comics and our unquenchable thirst for them all. One day, inspired by one of Oor Wullie's meditations on his bucket, I rounded up my pals and suggested that we each buy a different comic, and then swap them. I chose my favourite, the Hotspur, as it had everything I liked: stories about World War Two, cowboys, sports, and schoolboys, as well as fascinating historical accounts of real heroes like Scott, Livingstone and Edmund Hilary. Mintsy liked school stories, so he bought the Hornet as it had a great tale about a public school. Hogie liked blood and violence, so he opted for the Victor with its war stories. Having the most pocket money, Duffy had to buy two comics and we left him to choose between the Valiant, the Lion and the Eagle.

So we all started swapping our comics. These comics had their own particular style, but there was something in the drawings which united them. The heroes all had the same facial expressions, and they all had the same incredible mastery over their movements, enabling them to swerve, duck and punch with consummate ease. We tried to do the same, adopting impassive, fearless poses, ready to confront whatever horde of barbarians we encountered. We posed dramatically, holding imaginary rifles, knives and grenades. In our games we re-enacted everything we'd read, and everyone knew the appropriate stance and gesture required whether we were cigar-smoking American generals, or grinning Mexican bandits.

Then my brother started bringing home glossy American comics. The world they depicted was very different from that of chirpy schoolboys or valiant sergeants. This was a new world - a world of Superheroes! These were published by D.C. Comics, one of the oldest and largest American comic book producers. The shiny covers felt nice to touch, the drawings were spectacular, and the colours were amazing, and so much brighter than the cheap paper comics I was used to. The greatest superhero of them all, was, of course, Superman. My heroes in the Hotspur were like gnats compared to him. I became enthralled by his story and soon knew everything about his birth on planet Krypton, his journey to earth, and his life as reporter Clark Kent. His story made complete sense to me. I drank it all in: there was Superman, Superboy, Supergirl and even Superdog.

There were dozens of superheroes who each possessed extraordinary powers. The Flash ran like lightning, Wonder Woman had her magic lasso. Mintsy became our authority on Batman and Robin and Bruce Wayne's secret life in Gotham City. But for me, Batman and the other minor heroes paled in comparison with Superman and his superior powers.

Then things changed again with the arrival of Marvel Comics. Their heroes were different. They were not just 'goodies' fighting 'baddies'. They had complex personalities. Sometimes they were noble and heroic, but at other times they could be mean, depressed and confused. Spiderman was my favourite. He wasn't at all like the nice unassuming Clark Kent. Superheroes could be moody and self-pitying, not just dutiful and self-sacrificing. Something had happened. Superheroes had become...human! They could be weak and insecure, just like us.

These American comics didn't come out regularly but seemed to arrive in bulk in shiploads. Suddenly, there were all kinds of comics available at the same time. We quickly managed to acquire a number of them, and that's when our swapping system really developed. With only half a dozen comics each, we were soon able to access every comic in the neighbourhood.

On Saturdays we would swap the comics we had read

during the week. We would walk about with a pile of comics under our arm and consult each other as to what we had and what we wanted. I would swap a Batman for a Superman, or a Spiderman for a Fantastic Four. Nobody was a collector. It was a wonderful system allowing us to read hundreds of comics for an initial cost of only five or six titles. We became more sophisticated and started bartering, which took cunning as we had to know the value of every comic in the eyes of our pals. We would try to read their faces to gauge how eager they were to swap. So one could exchange one recent Superman for three lesser Superheroes. We were learning the art of trading. Eventually everyone knew everything there was to know about Superheroes.

Why were we so fascinated by them? We certainly couldn't have articulated our thoughts. To me they were simply great! I loved their superpowers and their fantastic costumes. They belonged to a different universe, and yet I felt close to them. Superman saved Lois Lane from collapsing buildings and rescued sky-divers whose parachutes had failed. Batman saved innocent victims under attack in the streets of Gotham City. Spiderman whizzed between tower blocks and caught falling children. They saved the poor, the weak and the helpless from the vile warlords and megalomaniacs who roamed the Marvel Comic universe.

Every Sunday, the priest told us that Our Saviour had sacrificed Himself to save our souls. But the Superheroes were our real saviours. They saved us from the grey monotony of our housing scheme. We were 'Valiant'. We were

'Victors'. Much later I learned that 'beano' actually means a happy state, a celebration, and a time of enjoyment. And indeed reading comics was one of the greatest enjoyments of my childhood.

Like Oor Wullie on his bucket, I felt like a king on a throne when I had a comic in my hand.

10. DRINK

One of the worst experiences of childhood can be witnessing unattractive adult behaviour. Adults are often at their worst when at home, unseen by the outside world. There they reveal the darker side of their nature to their children without realising the deep and lasting impact this can have. Stunned into submissive silence, children have to accept their parents' shameful behaviour.

Like most Easterhouse men, my Da was a worker who lived from week to week. He was paid on Fridays and we lived as best we could until the following pay-day. My parents rented a council flat. There was no mortgage, car, or savings, and no dreams, perhaps because Da had no ambition to live any better. He was a turner; a skilled worker who was at once proud of, and annoyed by his lot. He felt superior to unskilled and semi-skilled workers, and even white-collar staff, whom he called "wishy-washy pen-pushers". And he regarded the unemployed with utter scorn. Yet he was embittered and believed he deserved better in life. All this bottled-up anger, self-pity, and frustration was unleashed on pay-day. That's when he got steaming drunk.

I soon discovered that there were different kinds of

drunkenness, depending on a man's character, how they reacted to drink, and whether they knew when to stop. My Uncle Jerry was fabulous company after a few glasses. He joked and told stories and generously slipped us half-crowns. When tipsy at New Year, Auntie Kathleen joyfully sang and danced like Audrey Hepburn in *My Fair Lady.* And after a sherry or two Grandma forgot her worries and smiled benevolently at us from her armchair. Sometimes our neighbour, Mr. Nolan, smelled of drink when I met him in the Close, and he would smile and ruffle my hair, winking and joking.

Da was not like that. Sometimes he got tolerably drunk, which meant he could still walk. Collapsing into his armchair, he would listen to his Lonnie Donnegan records - *Last Train to Glasgow Central* - and ramble incoherently. But sometimes he got blind drunk, which Ma did not like. Neither did my brother and I. The awful thing was that we always knew when this would happen - we only had to look at the kitchen clock.

After school on a Friday afternoon I always felt happy at the prospect of the weekend ahead, reading comics, watching TV and playing football. However, after our 'tea' which we ate at about 5 o'clock, watching *Blue Peter*, the atmosphere would change. Around 5.30 we would start glancing furtively at the clock. If Da came back by 5.45, that meant he would have his dinner, give Ma his pay packet, have a wash and change, and go out to the pub at 7.30. No matter how much he drank after that, he wouldn't get totally plastered. But if he didn't come back by 5.45, that meant he had gone into the Brig Bar with his drinking mates on his way back from the station and, worst of all, with his pay packet.

When the minute hand reached 5.45 and we heard the door opening, we would sigh with relief. The gathering storm had lifted. But if the minute hand moved on to 6 o'clock, I would pray that the train was late and that the door would open at any moment. As the minute hand continued its relentless tick-tock, my heart fell further and I knew I had to brace myself for the inevitable.

There were two predictable endings to this plot: either go down to the pub to get Da, or go to Auntie Peggy's in Bridgeton. I hated the first option. Ma would become increasingly angry, smoking cigarette after cigarette. Finally, around 8.30 when her blood was 'boiling' and she could take no more, she would put on her coat, telling us to come with her to the pub. I was torn from the television to go to the last place in the world I wanted to be. I dragged my feet in shame behind Ma. Her aim was to stop him spending all his wages on drink. She knew that he could play 'the big man' and order 'drinks all round'. She knew that with every round of drinks he bought, she would have less money for the rent and food the following week.

The unwritten rule at that time was that a woman was not supposed to enter a bar to speak to 'her man' if he was with his drinking companions. That would be too humiliating for words. So Ma had to ask the barman at the 'carry-out' counter, which was separate from the bar area, to tell Da to come outside. Otherwise, she threatened to go in, dragging my brother and me behind her. I sunk into my duffle coat and tried to block out the world around me. There was a foul, sickly-sweet smell of beer and cigarette smoke, and a cacophony of drunk men shouting and jeering. I never dared to look at Da when he came out. But I heard Ma's restrained but angry voice and Da's grumbling as he spluttered out excuses, lurching around, trying to appear sober. Then she'd pull us away with her, gripping what remained of his pay packet. Although relieved to get away from the pub and glad that Ma had won her small victory, I knew that the evening was not over and that Da would come lumbering home in a foul temper after the pub shut.

So the second round of clock-watching began. This took into account the 10 pm closing time and the approximate time it took for a drunk man to walk home. This could be 15 to 40 minutes depending on his state and bouts of vomiting. As the clock moved on from 10.20 to 10.30 then 10.40 we could only expect the worst. My brother and I didn't go to bed on those nights. Finally we would hear a commotion on the first floor landing, signalling Da's approach. It sounded like a herd of cattle coming up the stairs. My father's mates usually bundled him up the Close, rang our bell and dropped him outside the door, leaving him sprawled against the coal cellar. Ma refused to open the door so my brother and I had to do it. He was a sorry sight and our neighbour, Mr McFadyen, the only man up the Close who didn't drink, would sometimes come out. He'd be annoyed by Da's disgraceful behaviour, and would take pity on us, helping us to bundle him into the flat. Da would then stagger into his bedroom and we prayed he would collapse on his bed and fall asleep. Sometimes he did, and we thanked the Lord for his drunken snoring. Sometimes he didn't, and then the situation became explosive. He would fumble about, propping himself up against the walls, then stagger into the kitchen or the toilet. When he came out, Ma would get it out of her system and call him all the names she could muster. He would wave her away imperiously. Ma thundered on, chain-smoking, puffing out her anger. My Da was not a violent man, and I never saw him strike her, but he would start roaring and arguing. I hunched my shoulders and cowered as the insults and bellowing resounded throughout the flat.

Unfortunately things sometimes deteriorated and something snapped in him. After being showered with insults he would turn on my brother and me, angry that we always seemed to take Ma's side. Our disapproving faces seemed like a betrayal by those for whom he claimed he worked his fingers to the bone day and night. Then my brother, who had become taller than Da, answered him back, and this led to pushing and shoving. I joined in, partly to separate them and partly to help my brother, grabbing Da's arm to restrain him. Sometimes this degenerated into a struggle with the three of us falling over each other on the sofa. Ma would scream blue murder and the neighbours would thump on their ceilings with broom handles, yelling at us to stop the racket or they would call the police. We always stopped before blood was spilt. My brother and I picked ourselves up and stood panting, glaring at Da who stayed slumped on the sofa with his head in his hands. He seemed to be struck dumb, lost in himself, knowing that he had behaved badly, and realising that he was rejected and despised. Then if it wasn't too late, Ma would make us put on our coats and we would take the last bus to Bridgeton to stay at Auntie Peggy's. Sometimes we went there before Da came back from the pub, and that's what I always hoped for. I could never understand why Ma put up with the arguing and fighting, when she could have avoided the fuss by simply leaving as soon as she got the remains of Da's wages.

Auntie Peggy was a spinster who lived alone with a cat in our deceased grandparents' home. I liked her as she was a kind of saviour from Da's drunkenness. She was also one of those nice adults we felt at ease with. She smiled and put her arm around us and made us feel welcome. I loved the sanctuary of her flat; it was so clean and quiet and safe. There were things that we didn't have like plants, nice carpets, old polished furniture and a sewing-machine. We drank tea and ate Tunnock's caramel wafers, even though it was late. Peggy had a very expressive face which registered shock, astonishment or joy at everything we said. I liked to sit and stroke her cat and listen to her endless gossip. Maybe it was because she lived alone, but whenever she was with Ma she couldn't stop talking, and you could hardly get a word in. She couldn't stand my Da, and neither could Ma's other sisters, Netty and Ruby. They were Protestants, and they lived differently from us. I once overheard Auntie Netty say that Da was "a selfish swine of a man," and she insinuated that all

Catholics were whingers and drunkards. What she really didn't like was that Da made Ma's life a misery. Catholics like Da were all spineless sinners to Netty; they were all destined for Hell. I agreed with her in part having seen the men in the pub, but I would be the first to admit there were a lot of Protestants there as well, knocking back the pints.

Netty was much tougher on Da than Peggy, who had a more forgiving nature. Netty was Ma's elder sister; older, wiser and much stricter in her Protestant values. She lived in a respectable part of Glasgow with her husband Glen, a quiet man who had a face like a Saint Bernard. Maybe that was because he was a teetotaler. When we visited them he would drink his tea in silence, while Netty talked incessantly. She was always very nice to us, and treated us like innocent victims. When she referred to Da, she used only his surname, to distance herself from him. Not only was he a drunk, he was a gambler too, and for Netty you couldn't get any worse.

It was true what she said about his drinking, but less so about the gambling, although he did like a bet. Opposite the pub was the bookies. Apart from drinking, that was Da's other pleasure. Whenever he had money it went on drink, or betting on horses or greyhounds. The pub and the bookies were houses of sin for Netty, but for Da they were houses of pleasure and escape. Like all the other flat-capped punters, he usually lost his money, but incredibly, a flicker of hope remained. And once in a blue moon he did actually win. If he won on a Saturday, he could go to the Club on Sunday, and spend his winnings on more drink. Pubs were closed on Sundays but so-called 'clubs' were open. These were drinking dens for members only. Perhaps his Catholic upbringing made him more restrained on a Sunday, as if God were keeping an eye on him. So he wouldn't get blind drunk, only totteringly tipsy. Or maybe it wasn't the reproachful eye of God which held him back, but the fact that the club closed at 2.30.

During the week he had no money, so he couldn't go to the pub. After his meal, he would sit in his armchair and watch the news, crime series or films. He seemed calm, but we couldn't disturb him or get in his way. He always decided what to watch on TV, and hardly said a word. It didn't occur to me to speak to him, and he never spoke to me. Ma usually stayed in the kitchen in the evening where she would read *The Daily Express* or *The Record*. I was puzzled that Da could be like teetotal Glen during the week, and then transform into a drunken wreck at the weekend. There was something of the 'Jekyll and Hyde' about him, brought on by "the Demon Drink" as Netty called it. And I didn't know which side of him was the real one. Was it the man sitting quietly watching TV, or was it the drunk sprawled outside our door on a Friday night? Was he living a lie like a double agent in a film?

Oddly enough, all the arguing and fighting was swept under the carpet the following day. A truce was reached, and as the youngest I was chosen to be the intermediary. This solemn ritual involved Ma making Da a cup of tea, and me reluctantly carrying the peace offering into the enemy lair. I walked slowly with my eyes riveted on the cup and saucer, my hands shaking, trying not to spill the tea. Inside the bedroom the curtains were drawn, and a bedside lamp was balanced precariously on a chair. I put the tea down beside the bed. Da was usually lying on his side with his back to the door so I couldn't see his face, and he would be reading an American paperback - *The Naked and the Dead* or *From Here to Eternity*. I had one thought in mind, and that was to get out of the room quickly. It stank of tobacco, beer and sweat. There were no friendly words or anything like an apology. "There's your tea, Da." I would say, and he would grunt "alright" without looking up from his book. And that was it. The page was turned. The storm had passed and life went on.

Da slept in the parental bedroom and Ma on the living room sofa, which folded down to become her bed. I never saw them talking or laughing together, let alone hugging, kissing, or even holding hands, gestures I saw in films and in the street. There was a black and white picture in an octagonal frame in the living room showing them standing side by side on their wedding day. Ma's wedding dress wasn't white, but an austere dark grey, more fitting for a funeral than a wedding. Ma had a ghost of a smile, but Da looked back stiffly as if he had been handed a life sentence. Perhaps this was a sign of things to come. I never once thought of my parents as a couple. They were two distinct individuals living their separate lives in the same small flat. I thought their relationship was normal as it was the only thing I knew. And yet I was seeing scenes in films and in books about happy mums and cheerful dads. Little by little, I began to think that there was something wrong in our place and that it was linked to what happened on Friday nights.

But there was nothing really unusual about my parents. Most of my pals' parents were the same. They didn't speak to us, and they didn't think of playing with us. None of them noticed us, except when we were in the way, and then they shouted. Adults gave nothing to their kids, so they got nothing back. We became as indifferent to them as they were to us.

Although I hated Da's drinking, life in Glasgow meant that I soon tasted the 'demon drink' myself. That was largely due to my pal, Frank Thompson, who got hold of cheap bottles of Madeira and sherry from his big brother, who organised discos at his college. Becoming a man meant smoking and drinking from the age of twelve or thirteen. But smoking was out of the question for me. My brother and I loathed anything to do with cigarettes. We had spent our childhood in a smoky atmosphere surrounded by ashtrays full of disgusting fag ends. But drinking was different. Although the initial taste was dreadful, we were soon giggling and doing stupid things. We passed the bottle around, slurping, choking and coughing. Our eyes were red, and we grinned inanely. Once I was stopped by a policeman who ticked me off for being drunk, then let me go after warning that he would tell my parents if he caught me again. Sadly he never did. And so, I went on, just like Da, drinking myself silly with my pals, until I threw up.

Ma was upset when she smelled the alcohol on my breath. I denied everything, saying it was a new sweet made from grapes. Then I tried to do handstands to prove I was sober, saying "Honest to God, I never had a drop". I was obviously too drunk to realise that a handstand was probably the last way to prove it. The hangover the next day was so bad that I wanted to wring my head off and throw it away. My brain was throbbing; I wailed with self-pity, and vowed never to drink again. But the week went by, Saturday arrived, and one of my mates produced a bottle and we all fell into the trap again. At the back of my mind I knew that drinking didn't 'make a man of you'. In fact, it did the opposite. It usually made you a bore. But at that time, for us, drinking meant getting drunk.

So how did our drinking really differ from Da's? For us it was a rite of passage. Looking back, I understand that Da drank to forget the past, to put off thinking about the future, but above all he drank to forget the present. He drank to forget who he was.

11. AIRFIX MODELS

Glasgow has a miserable, wet climate. Our vocabulary to describe rain is as rich as the Eskimo's for snow. When I was a child it was always spitting, drizzling, pouring, bucketing, pelting, lashing, or just pissing down. And it got dark very early from October to the end of February. In this gloomy, damp weather my cheap synthetic clothes were soon sodden, so I took refuge at home on wet and windy weekends. Apart from reading and watching TV, one of my main pastimes was re-enacting the war in the air. After I spent all my savings on the down-payment on my bike, I never regained my thriftiness. Whenever I got pocket money or a bung from Ma when she won at the bingo, or a postal order for my birthday, I would spend it on my new craze: building Airfix planes.

It was a very expensive hobby as I had to find the bus fare to go to Parkhead, there being no Woolworths in Easterhouse. Then I had to buy the kits, glue, paint brushes and paints to decorate them. Mintsy and Duffy came with me as we always shared our obsessions. Going to Woolworths was a treat for our impoverished eyes. We spent hours looking at the boxes on display, particularly the big ones showing giant coloured images of models which we could only dream of buying. High on the top shelf were models of enormous aircraft carriers and ocean liners like *The Queen Mary*. Even if we had been able to buy them, we wouldn't have known where to put them in our cramped bedrooms. There were Spanish galleons, Nelson's *Victory*, and ancient Greek warships with dozens of galley slaves. We acknowledged that these were fine models, but we were after only one thing. Given that we read the Hotspur and the Victor, we were only interested in World War Two.

So we focused on the heavy bombers: the Lancasters, Flying Fortresses and Junkers. They were our dream purchases, but given our budget of 2 shillings, we had to settle for smaller fry. Fortunately, Airfix had thought about us and produced something to match our budget. We began with the smallest and cheapest kits: fighter planes. Patriotically, we chose British planes to start our collections. I started with a Spitfire, Mintsy a Typhoon and Duffy a Hurricane. I liked the sound of the names. A plane that 'spits fire' reminded me of a dragon, and typhoons and hurricanes were devastating forces of nature, just like our planes. The men at the War Office were really pretty good at thinking up names for planes.

When I got home, I took out my box and looked at the cover, just as I had done all the way back on the bus. It showed a speedy, sharp-nosed Spitfire banking round to attack the German bomber in the corner of the picture. It was camouflaged in green and brown above, and blue underneath which really impressed me. And as I opened the box, I could almost hear Vera Lynn singing "There'll be bluebirds over the white cliffs of Dover..." and I could see young chaps scrambling into Spitfires to fight the Battle of Britain.

And then I opened the box and saw the bits of grey plastic stuck onto plastic rods. There were dozens of them: bits of fuselage, parts of wings, cockpit elements, wheels, gun turrets and some unidentifiable pieces. I felt the shock of reality - plastic reality. I had spent all my money on a pile of grey plastic. But after a moment's despair I began to study the assembly instructions. I read them again and again, and began to identify the parts, and with Vera Lynn warbling in my head, inspiring me to keep going, I took up the challenge and set to it. My first attempts at sticking the bits of plastic together were a total disaster. I stuck my thumb to my forefinger with no difficulty, but I couldn't manage to get the appropriate blobs of glue into the holes and the edges of the plane parts. Either there was too much and the glue dripped everywhere, or there wasn't enough and the parts limply fell apart.

I carried on doggedly, and finally assembled the fuselage, and the wings were almost straight. It began to look like an aeroplane. The rest took hours, particularly the tiny bits like the wheels, guns and cockpit. Finally, I finished the first part of the operation. I let the glue dry before painting the plane, and then completed the model with the red, white and blue insignia of the R.A.F. and the plane's identification numbers. My pile of plastic had been transformed into a redoubtable flying machine. I felt proud as I held it up, my fingers blackened with patches of dried glue and covered in paint. I had made it. I deserved a medal!

I decided to use my brother's bed as a landing strip (my own bed was a fold-up one in a cupboard). I gave the warning signal calling all pilots to scramble. My fingers ran quickly along the bed and jumped into my Spitfire. The engine roared and it took off. I raised it high in the air and it coasted through the skies seeking the enemy, then suddenly, on spotting German bombers near the window, I turned and bore down on them, firing all the machine guns at once. The bomber burst into flames and plummeted to the ground with a thick trail of black smoke. My first kill! The battle raged on. I shot down another three Heinkels while being hit in the tail by a rear gunner. Finally, I had to go back to base to refuel and re-arm. I landed on my brother's bed, told the mechanics to repair my tail wing and went off to have a cup of tea and a biscuit before taking off again. But there was a problem. I realised that I needed a real enemy. I needed a German plane.

So as soon as I could I went back to Woolworths. To my dismay, I couldn't afford a Stuka dive bomber and had to content myself with a Focke Wulf, a nondescript plane compared to the Stuka with its strange angled wings. I painstakingly went through the whole assembly business again, but this time I knew what to expect, and I went about it more quickly and methodically although I was just as awkward with the glue. And so began an evening of ferocious dogfights. I danced about with my Spitfire in one hand and the Focke Wulf in the other. They put on an incredible display of aerial gymnastics, zooming up and down, swerving right and left, narrowly missing collisions and looping the loop. Mrs Lynch downstairs thumped on her ceiling with her broomstick, calling for an end to the hostilities. The sound of the broomstick was like an anti-aircraft gun. Finally, I jumped off the bed and landed both planes, placing them on their plastic display stands with their noses turned proudly skyward. "The battle is over," I declared, "but not the war!"

In the weeks and months that followed I built up a considerable collection of model planes. Every penny I had was spent in Woolworths. I bought the Hurricane and Typhoon to join my Spitfire. And to match my glorious squadron of British fighters I acquired the fiendishly fast Messerschmitt with its unusual spotty camouflage, and, thanks to a few shillings from Ma's bingo winnings, my own Stuka. Although the Germans were the enemy, I had a healthy respect for their war machines. In war film after war film and in a thousand stories in my comics, I had seen the might of the *Luftwaffe* during the Blitz and in the Atlantic. So I put on my German accent and offered running commentaries on the dogfights between our chirpy British pilots and the Hauptmann Von Reichstag:

"Ve haf spotted Schpitfire. Achtung! Achtung!..."

"Look out chaps. Hun at 10 o'clock coming in from the East...Let's show the blighters what we're made of."

"Himmel, ve vill kaput you!"

"Bad news chaps, damn Hun has hit me, but just you wait. I swear I'll get that beastly Nazi!"

"Gott in Himmel! Ve haf been hit. Ve are kaput!"

And both planes descended to the decreasing drone of my voice, followed by two bangs to mark the end of the dogfight.

I realised that I needed reinforcements so I went back to Woolworths to help our war effort. We needed the Americans. I bought an American Mustang which I particularly liked because of the shark's teeth markings on the nose. I added a sturdy Curtiss Tomahawk for support. I had a strong sense of fair play when it came to combat. So I sportingly offered the Axis Forces a Japanese Kawasaki fighter and the infamous suicide bomber, the Mitsubishi Zero, with its terrifying red circle insignia; the 'rising sun'. The war was heating up. But more was to come.

Fighter planes were all very well, but the real instruments of victory in war were the bombers. I had seen the American films *Flying Fortress* and *The Wild Blue Yonder* showing the Boeing giants, which seemed as big as football fields. And I'd seen *The Dambusters* where British boffins ingeniously invented a bouncing bomb - only the cricket-playing English could have thought of that - to explode against a seemingly impregnable dam. These films inspired me. My first bomber was a Lancaster Dambuster. It took ages to build and it made my Spitfire look like a fly.

I only flew it at night. I put out the bedroom light and raised my arm as high as I could to lift my Lancaster into the upper altitude. I used my torch to represent searchlights guiding the anti-aircraft gunfire. But they could not destroy my bomber. It released its deadly cargo and I symbolically extinguished my torch.

But the Germans wanted revenge. So back to Woolworths I went and bought a Junkers. It was not as big as the Lancaster, but it looked fierce and powerful. So night after night I re-enacted the war in the air over Europe. My dream of acting out the war in the Pacific was not to be, as I couldn't afford an American Flying Fortress. So, my little Mitsubishi Zero had the run of the skies. Then one weekend, worn out by my aerial combat, I decided to end the war. My Lancaster flew on a final raid over Germany, the enemy capitulated, and a peace treaty was signed on my brother's bed.

But what was I to do now with all my planes? I had no place to store them in my bedroom. Then I had a brainwave; I would put them where they belonged - in the sky! So with the help of my brother, I stood on a stepladder and attached my planes with sellotape, string and tacks to the ceiling of our room. I didn't want a predictable line-up of British and Americans on one side and the Germans and Japanese on the other. So I mixed them up to look like dogfights between enemy fighters, and bombers under attack. My dull white ceiling now looked dramatic. I put on a special show for my pals, who were all impressed, particularly when I put the light off, and shone two torches onto the ceiling while imitating the sound of anti-aircraft gunfire.

I felt that I should be interested in model ships because Ma had told me Da had been in the Navy and had even gone to South Africa at the end of the war. Woolworths had all kinds of battleships, aircraft carriers, and destroyers surging across the Atlantic, canons blazing. I needed expert advice to help me choose, so one evening I decided to ask Da. He was sitting in his armchair, smoking and watching a crime serial. Normally, I wouldn't interrupt him. In fact I would never dream of speaking to him, nor he to me, but when the adverts came on, it seemed like an opportune moment. The words popped out of my mouth:

"Da, I was thinking of buying a ship." I said.

"What?" he grunted back, surprised no doubt that I was speaking to him. "A ship?"

"Aye...A model ship. At Woolworths. Airfix, you know. Just like my planes."

"Your planes?"

"Aye, in our room...Have you not seen them?"

He didn't reply. He never came into the room I shared with my brother. I had never asked him if he wanted to see my planes. He continued watching the adverts "I don't know what kind of boat to buy." I continued, and ventured, "What were you on in the Navy?" I hoped he would tell me that he'd been a gunner on a destroyer, or the captain of a mine-sweeper.

"Just a boat." he answered, and took a drag on his cigarette.

"Was it a destroyer?" I persevered.

"No, it was just...just a big boat...You know..."

I didn't know. 'Big' meant nothing to me. I wanted details. I was about to ask him to explain the difference between a cruiser and a destroyer, but I thought better of it. Then I made a mistake. I asked the wrong question.

"Did you ever sink any German boats?"

He sighed, exasperated; he said "You're joking. I was just in the..."

Then the detective story came on again.

"Look." he said, his eyes still on the TV. "I'll tell you some other time about all that."

But he never did. And I never asked him again. I dropped the idea of buying an Airfix boat.

But my plastic wars didn't stop there. I felt it was time to wage some land warfare. Beside the Airfix planes kits in Woolworths was another section devoted to toy soldiers. There were all kinds: U.S. Marines, German mountain troops, Japanese infantry, and so on. The choice was incredible. I decided to quit Europe, and, since it was a World War, to head for the desert. So I bought the British Eighth Army, and also their fearsome enemy, the German Afrika Korps.

Back home, I studied the picture on the Eighth Army box. Here was a British soldier with glinting eyes and a set jaw, dressed in khaki shorts, dashing through a cloud of billowing sand, pointing a rifle with fixed bayonet. Alongside him was an officer holding up his revolver and urging his company to charge. On the Afrika Korps box, the men looked intimidating, with their grim faces and swastika-covered tanks. They were exactly like the images in my favourite comics. I was in my element.

But when I opened the box I experienced the same initial disappointment I had felt with my first Spitfire. The soldiers were so tiny! Not even an inch high. I unpicked them from their plastic rods and lined up my army of midgets. There were two or three armed soldiers for each posture: standing, kneeling, crawling or lying down. None was dying or surrendering! It was only when I moved them into position that they began to spark into life. Suddenly, I imagined the sun was beating down and the Eighth Army was on the move across the desert. I was leading my men through minefields and crawling up sand dunes on the folds of the sheets on my brother's bed. With Rommel's Afrika Korps set out on the carpet, the battle was ready to begin. Like a God, I sent both armies into combat. And like a God, I tipped the men over when they were dead. I played with my tiny soldiers, but I had to admit that my heart wasn't in it. I needed more soldiers, and perhaps some different armies.

So I went back to Woolworths to buy a box of U.S. Marines. To my surprise, I found three men were looking at the boxes at the Airfix counter. I thought they must be nice fathers, come here to buy some kits for their kids. My Da would never have done that. And then one of them spoke to the others about "the exciting news" that Airfix had just brought out a new series featuring the Australian infantry. And they were planning to produce the Burmese Army Corps before Christmas. He couldn't wait to see it. Then they began to discuss model sizes, comparing 1/32 scale to 1/72 which fascinated them. They didn't notice me. I thought they were intruders on my territory, but in fact this was their patch. It seemed that Airfix soldiers were designed for adults who got a kick out of buying these plastic reproductions. I saw them as toys to be brought to life through play, but these guys were collectors who filled their shelves with collections of soldiers arranged in orderly formation.

When I got home I didn't want to play anymore. I still admired the planes suspended above me and the steadfast soldiers of the Eighth Army spread out on the carpet, but now I saw them differently. Some of the magic had gone. I no longer needed plastic armies.

The following Saturday I didn't go to Woolworths.

It's strange to think that I spent so much of my childhood with a weapon in my hand. Whether I was Robin Hood with a bow and arrow, Geronimo with a hatchet or James Bond with a revolver, I was always running around slaughtering people. Between the ages of five and nine, we played endless games of cops and robbers, cowboys and Indians, 'Japs' and commandos; every variation of goodies versus baddies. At that age I used my finger and thumb as a gun more than I used them to hold a pen. I shot at everything that moved and my pals did the same. I loved killing, of course, but I had a great fondness for dying as well. I don't know how many times I died as a kid. It became an art. Falling over, riddled with bullets, or being shot by arrows like Saint Sebastian; this was my daily lot. I would stagger forward clutching my bleeding chest, looking up with an anguished expression before finally dropping to my knees and keeling over with outstretched hands. I was looking for applause from my pals for my dramatic death throes.

I remember watching the Beatles on TV when they were in their hippie period just before the *Sergeant Pepper* album. They were in the recording studio, clapping their hands, and chanting "All we are saying is... Give Peace a Chance." I didn't understand. I had been brought up on killing and war. But I liked John Lennon. He was funny and irreverent. So I started humming the refrain in my head. The next day, my pals and I shuffled about the playground with short Hare Khrishna steps, clapping our hands above our heads and chanting: "All we are say-ing is...give peace a chance". We wanted everyone to join in, but the girls just giggled. We eventually gave up as even we got bored with our monotonous chanting. Then Hogie started again, only this time, chanting "All we are say-ing... is give *War* a chance!" We all laughed - we thought we were hilarious - and then we pulled out our knives and guns and started gleefully slaughtering each other again.

Miss Markey said that one of the best and longest novels was *War and Peace*. I liked the title. I asked her if she had read it, and she looked at me the way Da had done when I asked him if he had sunk any German ships. Later in life, when I came to read the novel, I couldn't help thinking about my passion for warfare as a child despite living in a period of peace in Europe. War was dreadful, and yet it was the inspiration for all our games.

For me it was not so much a question of *War and Peace*, but *War then Peace*. Having enjoyed years of imaginary warfare, I had finally grown out of it. The planes went back in their boxes.

12. THE LOCH

Easterhouse was built from scratch on windswept fields to the east of Glasgow. Around the hundreds of breeze-block tenement buildings was a strange mixture of wild fields, agricultural land, abandoned industrial sites, woodland and lochs. From the age of six I began my first expeditions beyond the boundaries of the scheme. The nearest place was behind Denmilne Street. This was simply called 'The Fields' where we found ourselves in open countryside. In the uncultivated fields there were mounds of earth, rocks and pebbles, covered in grass and weeds. I was told that these were the remains of the construction work done when the housing scheme was built in the late nineteen-fifties. The builders had just dumped the rubble in the surrounding fields. For environmentalists with today's perspective this was irresponsible; for small boys like me and my pals, these mounds were fabulous. We ran up and down them and practised dare-devil stunts on our bikes. We played 'king of the castle', pushing and shoving one another off the top, to stand alone as the mighty king surveying his realm.

There was an almost level stretch of land where we played 'serious' football. This meant eleven of us making up a full team to play against teams from neighbouring streets. Oddly enough I preferred playing football in the swing-park. The Fields meant something else for me and the rules of football seemed out of place in this rough wilderness.

Sometimes we would see greyhounds racing on training runs. The dog-breeders were hard-looking men who lined up their dogs in makeshift traps then released them to fly like the wind chasing a wooden hare pulled by a cord. Greyhound racing was a minor but popular sport at the time. Da used to bet on the dogs, and sometimes I watched greyhound racing on TV. But nothing seen on a flickering screen compared to the breathtaking sight of the dogs close up, bolting through the fields.

When we were around nine, and more self-assured, we ventured beyond the fields, over the Monkland Canal, up towards Bargeddie Church and Coatbridge. Sometimes we walked for hours over countryside and saw no one. But woodland and barley fields didn't interest us. We liked the abandoned junk on the brownfield sites, and the derelict railway lines leading to rusting corrugated-iron warehouses. There were piles of scrap iron, broken tiles and pipes and heaps of shale covered in weeds and this-tles. We didn't know at the time, but we were looking at the remains of the industrial revolution which had made Glasgow rich a century before. Our favourite place was an abandoned train with three wagons at the end of a railway siding. They had been smashed up, but we found it exciting to imagine we were on the *Orient Express* or crossing the American plains to strike gold in California.

We never stayed too long in the train or in the run-down warehouses. We felt uneasy, and we often spoke in whispers. There was something eerie about these places. We sensed the presence of past lives in the debris around us.

There was no motorway between Glasgow and Edinburgh at that time, just the Edinburgh Road, which became an important landmark. We usually wandered around the fields and quiet country roads to its north, but sometimes we crossed it, and walked warily, like cowboys entering outlaw territory. We tried to avoid groups of boys, especially older ones. One time when we were exploring the fields around Hamilton, two older boys appeared and one of them started prodding Hogie in the chest, saying "Where do you think you're going, shitface?" While he held our attention, the other kid came up behind me and smashed an egg on my head. They both exploded with laughter and then walked away, telling us to get the hell out of their place. I was shaking with rage. I would rather have been kicked or punched. An egg cracked on your skull was too demeaning for words. We didn't cross the Edinburgh Road again, and it became a hard border. We stayed on its north side, which turned out to be a good decision for that was where the lochs were. They became our favourite haunt at weekends and during the summer holidays.

Around that time I noticed that Miss Markey had become awfully fat. One day she told us she had to leave for a while, but she would be back in a few months. I imagined that she was going on a strict diet. In the meantime she would be replaced by Miss Savage who would be in class the next day. We were terrified. Miss Savage! What had we done to deserve such a fate? What was in store - torture for those who got their sums wrong? Then Miss Savage appeared. We scarcely dared lift our eyes, but Miss Savage was smiling, she had soft blue eyes and a soft voice. She was much nicer-looking than Miss Markey and she wore a stroke-able pink woollen pullover. She was no savage.

There was to be no torture. Instead she told us that we were going to study "the wonders of nature". We looked at each other: what was that? She began to tell us about natural cycles, and that animals reproduced. She introduced us to the term "a fight for survival" in the natural world. We understood that! She showed us pictures of animals, flowers and trees. They were all fighting to survive, and they all had incredible powers to resist their natural enemies, which seemed to include just about every other species. Life was a battlefield. What troubled us was that at the end of the day, few survived. A fish had two thousands eggs, and only ten survived. What about the others? Miss Savage said "That's life." You call that life, I thought. Being born to die? I couldn't quite take it in.

She talked about the "beauty of nature". Plants and animals knew how to attract one another, and the more attractive they were the better their chance of survival. We all looked at Hogie. We sighed - the poor devil. He was surely condemned to extinction. Miss Savage concluded by saying that we were all going to study Nature and discover for ourselves what life was all about. We happily agreed; at last we would have an answer.

"Let's begin with bees," she announced. This was right up our street. We knew they could be found in the Fields. Sometimes they stung us when we ran about or played football. It was time for revenge. This was 'survival of the fittest' after all. This was 'us or them'! I raised my hand to say, "We know where we can get you some bumble bees, Miss." Her face brightened; she couldn't believe her nature classes could excite such enthusiasm.

"Do you want them dead or alive, Miss?" I asked.

Her face squirmed. "Alive, of course. We want to *observe* nature's creatures, not kill them."

"Understood, Miss." I replied, remembering the horrendous drowning experiments we had conducted on bees that we'd caught. We were going to change. We were going to become scientists and *observe* Nature.

One of the consequences of the huge number of 'jeely pieces' that kids consumed at the time was the number of jam jars everyone acquired. Parents used them to store buttons and nails and so on. We used them to catch bees, butterflies and insects.

Carrying two or three each, we went to the Fields on our hunting expedition. The bees had no chance. Moving stealthily through the clumps of grass and weeds, we crouched beside the unsuspecting bees and plunged our jam jars down to trap them. We screwed on the lids and watched the poor things crawling around inside. The first scientific discovery we made was that bees need oxygen. We had irrefutable proof of this, as all of our bees died. So Hogie pulled out his flick-knife and stabbed the jam jar lids to let in air. We started afresh on our hunt, and soon we had amassed a fine collection of bees, wasps, hornets and something we called 'red-hot pokers' because of their yellow-orange tails. No one was stung, and we congratulated ourselves on our hunting prowess, thinking of the triumphant entrance we would make the next day in class. The droning and buzzing reverberated in the jars as we walked home.

Next day the jam jars were silent. Two bees bumbled about listlessly. The wasps and hornets lay rigid and the red-hot pokers were just blackened remains. Our second scientific discovery: wasps and bees need food. Nevertheless we decided to take them to school to impress the girls. But sadly neither the girls nor Miss Savage were remotely impressed by our collection of corpses.

Miss Savage asked about the kind of flowers which attracted bees, which part of the flower the bees focused on, and what they did with their legs when crawling inside the flower. We were stumped. It turned out we were more hunter than scientist. The girls laughed at our ignorance because they knew the answers. They had simply found them in books without observing the bees at work. We were underappreciated. Had we not risked being stung? Had we not kept our word and brought specimens in near perfect condition - if a trifle dead - for the nature study? Seeing that we were peeved, Miss Savage said she wanted to open up our study to include water life. Did any of us know where we could find frogs and tadpoles? I raised my hand, bursting to say I knew where to get some. "We'll bring you some on Monday," I declared proudly. We had a mission that Sunday. We had to go to The Loch.

Before we set off, Duffy asked, "How do you tell the difference between an Englishman and a Scotsman?" We shrugged. "Ask them to say *loch*." he replied, "No English person can say it correctly." Duffy had actually been to visit his family in England so we believed him. He pouted his lips, put on a funny accent and said "Lock Lomond." Then he said in his most guttural Scottish accent, "Locchh Lomond".

We all did the same with a grating rattle in our throats. Maybe all the Barr's Irn-Bru we drank helped. 'Loch' was an important word for me. I lived in *Loch*dochart Road. That was a bit of a mystery as I had walked all the way up and down it without seeing any loch. I asked my brother where it was, and he told me I was a twit, and that it didn't exist. Then he told me about the local lochs within walking distance. Lochend Loch, Bishop's Loch, Drumpellier Loch and others. We set out to visit them. Our outings always began with our guttural cry; "Let's go up the Locchh"

Drumpellier had the easiest access. We went up a country road that wound through woodland and fields before arriving at the loch, which was completely wild with no paths, car parks or any amenities. It was surrounded by sharp-bladed grass and bushes. The constant wind rippled the freezing, dull-grey water. Sometimes we'd encounter a couple of fishermen, who would glare at us when they saw us coming.

Miss Savage had asked us to observe Nature and now we did so religiously, bowing our heads over the banks and silently peering through the grass into the shallow water. We soon heard the gurgling call of frogs and toads. We weren't very good at identifying things in nature. We had no vocabulary to describe the world around us. Oaks, birches and beech trees were words I encountered only in books. We couldn't name the multitude of plants and trees which we saw, but Miss Savage was to change all that.

Toads disgusted us, but at the same time, we had a childish fascination for all that repels. The toads could be found bobbing about with their revolting heads and glaucous eyes breaking the surface. They opened their mouths and burped and croaked and we copied them. Hogie snorted and farted and growled and croaked like a demented reptile. The toads seemed to appreciate this, as they croaked all the more.

We stuck our hands in the water and swished them about until we felt a gluey mass of frogspawn. We pulled out the translucent blob with its tiny black spots trembling inside. I had a strange feeling - was I linked to the frogspawn? Did all forms of life have something in common? But Hogie started croaking again, dispelling my thoughts. We stuffed the frogspawn into a bucket and set about catching tadpoles. They were darting about at the water's edge and we caught hundreds of them. We shrieked with the excitement of the catch. The fishermen watched us grimly from the other side of the loch.

On Monday, we proudly displayed our catch to the teacher, but actually we were trying to impress the girls. We had gone to a distant land and battled the elements to bring back this precious bounty for them to feast their eyes upon. We showed them our half-dead tadpoles wriggling lamely in the jam jars, and one mute toad which looked back glumly from his glass jail. Sadly, the girls remained unimpressed but Miss Savage congratulated us on our exploits. Then she began to tell us about things we couldn't, or perhaps didn't want to think about; frogs came together with other frogs of the opposite sex to make frogspawn. "And we are the same", she said. It was called the "cycle of life". So I was linked to the frogspawn after all!

I raised my hand and asked Miss Savage what she would like us to bring next. We knew of a place in Lochend where swans laid eggs, and where coots, mallards and moorhens built their nests. We could swipe a few eggs, study them and then take them back if she wished. Hogie sprang up to tell her about a fox's lair he had heard about, so perhaps we could have fox cubs in the classroom to play with. The girls began to look interested.

Miss Savage calmed him down, and said that our role was to respect nature, not to disturb its mysterious workings by stealing eggs or offspring. We should be privileged onlookers of the world around us. She added that we should open our hearts to whatever we saw, whether a bee buzzing on a flower or a toad croaking its aria in a pond. We had to look and feel, not intervene and steal. I liked what she was saying, but I was not convinced. My world was one of boys and girls, adults and children, catholics and protestants, rich and poor; it was a binary existence. Peaceful co-existence and mutual understanding seemed far from our world.

My exploration of the natural world had some setbacks. One summer day when for once the sun shone over Glasgow, we couldn't resist taking off our shoes and paddling in the loch. Thinking it would be like the swimming pool, we waded gormlessly into the cold water. We found ourselves squelching in a swampy mud bath. Suddenly I felt something solid under my feet, something sharp and hard. I winced and came out to find a trail of blood streaming from my muddy left foot. I must have stood on a broken bottle or a tin. We set off home, me limping as I clung to Mintsy and Duffy. Two cars passed, but they didn't stop in spite of our pleading. Finally, we got back to my place and Duffy explained to Ma what had happened. She complained about having to buy me a new pair of socks and shoes. The ambulance took me to the doctor's surgery where a nurse stitched up the gash. She said I was lucky. I only needed six stitches.

My pals were impressed when I showed them the stitches. We were all proud of our scars. I had them all over my body. Ten stitches on my forehead, three on my knee and four on my right hand from falls in the swingpark. So now I had stitches on my foot, too. I felt like a gladiator. The only problem was that I couldn't play football for a month, but on the other hand my acting improved tremendously. I dragged my foot behind me as I entered the classroom, grimacing like a wounded war hero. From time to time I would bend to rub my foot, to show Ann Bolan how much pain I was in. Sometimes I lifted my eyes upwards as if begging the Almighty to take pity upon his devoted subject and alleviate his suffering.

But Ann Bolan never looked my way. And then I understood: girls, and particularly the pretty ones, don't like lame ducks. They were only interested in men of action. Miss Savage was right. It was 'survival of the fittest'. I stopped playacting and resolved to get over my injury as fast as possible.

Looking back, I didn't realise that roaming in unfamiliar territory would toughen and embolden me. What I liked was the contrast with the familiar patterns of daily life. Exploring beyond our housing scheme was satisfying; I enjoyed being out in the open and I enjoyed the journey as much as the destination. The sky and the road seemed endless, and the waters of the loch infinite. They made me think about the story of Jesus walking on water: I imagined walking on these waters, and the waters of the loch taking me to a better life, somewhere else.

The loch was constant, a strange watery mass which was there before me and which would be there long after I had gone. Miss Savage taught us the words of *The Bonnie Banks of Loch Lomond*. I liked the lines: "I'll tak' the high road and you'll tak' the low road…".

So there was more than one road. I felt sure that whether I took the high or the low one, it would lead me somewhere bonnie.

13. HOLIDAYS

'Holidays' was a magical word for me as a child. It meant not having to go to school. There were also the 'Holy Days' when we Catholics didn't go to school, although we had to go to mass. Being on holiday meant seemingly endless days, playing or exploring with my pals, or reading on my own. Going on holiday was different. Those were the rare moments when I found myself in a strange place with my family, but without my pals. There were two holidays I remember. One was a trip to Saltcoats, about fifty miles to the south of Glasgow on the west coast of Ayrshire. The other was a trip to Port Seton, a small town near Edinburgh, which overlooks the Firth of Forth. Port Seton perhaps had the biggest impact on me as it was the first time I saw the sea.

When I discovered we were going to the seaside at Port Seton I was very excited. I had seen holiday programmes showing beautiful white sandy beaches under a scorching sun. There were men with rippling muscles, and women like Goddesses, who reclined under parasols, sipping long drinks. Everyone was gloriously tanned with brilliant white teeth. They played beach tennis or sun bathed, and afterwards these sun-soaked lotus-eaters would retire to their exclusive hotels to lounge beside fabulous swimming pools. I boasted to my pals that I was off for a week of luxury in a five star hotel and that I would return sun-tanned like a film star. Then Ma told me that we weren't actually going to a hotel, but to a house with a garden! That seemed even better to me. After climbing up and down the stairs in our Close for as long as I could remember, I was enchanted by the idea of being in a house where I could open the front door and step outside. I imagined that the house would have a stunning view of the sea, and the garden would have a perfect lawn where I could run around and play football.

When we arrived at our holiday home, I discovered our 'house' was, in fact, a hut. A ramshackle hut beside other dark green and brown wooden huts on a windswept campsite. There were iron bunk beds covered in rough grey blankets like in a prisoner of war camp. There was no bath or hot water. There was a patch of rough grass enclosed by a broken fence. That was the 'garden'. The toilet was a tiny wooden shed in the back garden. No running water meant no flush toilet. So a man came every two or three days with a horse and a cart to empty the bucket in the shed. We called him 'the manure man' and we voted his job the worst in the world. His horse was the most forlorn creature I had ever seen. It wore black blinkers and its head was permanently bowed as if waiting to be guillotined. It stank to high heaven, and so did its master and his cart. After being 'cleaned' the toilet was still a nightmare place. Suddenly our flat in Easterhouse seemed quite attractive.

We went to Port Seton with our ground floor neighbours, the Hamiltons, who rented a nearby hut just as
awful as ours. Mrs. Hamilton was company for Ma. Mr.
Hamilton sometimes joined us, but often he went on long
walks on his own. I never saw my Da. He was always at
the pub. I was supposed to play with the Hamilton children, David, Ann and Thomas, but it was difficult as Ann
and David were a lot younger than me and Thomas was
severely handicapped and had learning disabilities. Fortunately, there was the seaside. I couldn't wait to go. But
I was told the beach was for the following day as it was
raining when we arrived, and Ma wanted to get settled in.
I didn't know where to go, and found myself on the rough
grass wasteland in front of our hut. It was cold, wet and
miserable outside and cold, damp and miserable inside. I
shivered in my new red-hooped T-shirt, wondering what
to do. I tried to play football with Thomas and Ann but
there was no fun in dribbling around a four-year-old girl.
The kids were a bit listless and I tried to play at all sorts of
games with them, but they just hung awkwardly. I sorely
missed my pals.

Wherever I looked, everything was new and different.
There were lots of other huts and children like me,
equally lost for something to do with themselves in such
a strange place. We clung onto the wooden fences around
our huts as if they would protect us. That was my initial
feeling about holidays; they were a bit frightening at first;
a foreign territory, living at a different pace, and irregular
mealtimes and bedtimes. Every door opened differently,
the light switches were hard to find, the chairs were too

big and there were piles of mismatched plates and cups in the cupboards.

The next day was cold and windy with heavy glowering clouds thudding across the sky. But it wasn't raining, and in Scotland we call that a great day. So we went to the beach. It took ages to walk to the seashore, but on we went with our bags, buckets and spades. I could smell the sea before I could see it. It was a pungent salty smell like the inside of a packet of salt and vinegar crisps. Huge seagulls were screeching and whirling in the sky, which made Thomas giggle hysterically. I was tense with excitement as we finally crossed the coast road and saw the sea.

It was a dismal sight. No palm trees, no white sand, no blue sea, no beautiful sun-tanned bathers. This was not the beach I had imagined. We looked out upon a wind-swept expanse of pebbles, patches of sand, rough grass, seaweed, and rock pools. The sea was dark grey. On the horizon was a dark bluish line which seemed to be land. "That must be Kirkcaldy on the other side of the Forth" said Mr. Hamilton, who had come with us. My Da wasn't there as predictably he had gone to the pub. I then understood that we weren't really at the seaside, but at the mouth of the Forth Estuary. We spotted some boats in the far distance which cheered me up. I had never seen a real boat before. I imagined Spanish galleons or the Cutty Sark speeding over the waves to China. Excited, I asked Mr. Hamilton what they were. "Oil tankers" he said in his matter-of-fact voice, "Oil tankers going to the refinery at Grangemouth."

It was deserted except for a man walking two dogs by

the shore. Mr. Hamilton led us down through the clumps of grass, warning us to be careful as it could cut us to shreds. Fortunately, Ma had bought me a pair of plastic sandals. Without them my feet would have been lacerated by the broken shells and pebbles, which Mr. Hamilton called 'shingle'. Tripping over rocks and seaweed, we ran to the seashore and began to paddle in the sea. The water was freezing. My feet went livid and I trembled with the shock of each step. We began stamping our feet and splashing as the waves broke around our ankles. Mr. Hamilton shouted to us to come and change as we still had our clothes on. We rushed back, tore off our clothes and put on our swimming trunks. My brother led the way and I held Ann by the hand as we edged into the lapping waves. No one dared to go further than knee-high. We were shivering, but tingling with excitement too. We started jumping up and down and running into the waves. Splashing and kicking the water warmed us up, so we bobbed up and down, running in and out of the breaking waves. I remember stopping at one point, my ears full of water, and feeling dizzy. My eyes swept the immense horizon and I felt very tiny in this vast space. But I was quickly startled back to the moment by Mr. Hamilton, now in his swimming trunks, throwing handfuls of wet sand at me. We all started throwing sand at one another, shrieking like seagulls. The sea had become a mud bath, and we were wild primitive creatures dancing in the squelchy brown sand.

Whatever the weather, we would spend a couple of hours each day at the beach, splashing about, exploring the rock pools and collecting shells. We also went to the port and looked at the brightly coloured fishing boats and the fishermen in their yellow oilskins. That's where I discovered the Scottish alternative to a breakfast of soggy cornflakes: kippers. Ma bought some at the port and served them up the next morning. I loved their smokey saltiness. I lifted the fishbone in one piece and wiggled it like a Halloween skeleton. Unfortunately, the smell of the fried fish lingered in the hut for the rest of the week.

I was a little older when we visited Saltcoats. I had learned to swim by then, or at least thought I could until I went into the sea. We had gone with the Nolans from our Close. They had two children; Patricia, who was two years older than me and Peter, who was two years younger. Patricia stuck with my brother while I got stuck with Peter. He clung to me all the time as if we might abandon him to the seagulls. Unlike Port Seton, Saltcoats had a real beach with a sandy stretch free from rocks and shingle. I decided to try to swim, and as Peter looked on anxiously, with his small screwed-up eyes, I moved further out until the water was up to my chest. Shivering with cold, I bounced up and down to keep my head above water as I did at the swimming pool, but this was different. Suddenly I could hear nothing except the sound of my own gulping as I panted for air. Peter's tiny face seemed to get smaller and smaller. He was shouting something but I couldn't hear him. Then a wave walloped me on the back, lifted me up and swept me out of my depth.

I had swallowed a lot of sea water and began to choke and splash about as I tried to keep swimming. Another wave hit me and I was carried further from the shore. I was panicking; beneath my thrashing legs was a cold watery emptiness. I knew I was incapable of getting back to the shore. I was terrified that I was going to drown. I had the same feeling that I'd experienced at Port Seton; I felt insignificant and vulnerable. I was lost in the midst of the vast emptiness of sea and sky. And I heard a terrifying voice in my head gravely intoning: "Out of the depths I have cried to thee, O Lord...Lord, hear my voice..." It was *De Profundis*, the prayer we had learned by heart for our Confirmation. I was literally out of my depth, and I was crying out to be saved. I could sometimes glimpse the shore, but most of the time I was lost in the swell of the sea, which pulled me this way and that. My mind went blank.

Then I was coughing and spluttering on the beach. I had a towel over my shoulders and everyone was laughing and asking if I was alright. "You've drunk so much water, it looks like the tide's gone out" Mr. Nolan joked. It turned out that Peter had alerted his sister and she had swum out and pulled me to safety. She teased me, saying her dog was a better swimmer than me. She ruffled my hair and said I was a "wee daftie", and I had better take more care before plunging back into the sea. I was grateful and promised I would never try that again. "Wait till we tell your father." Mr. Nolan added, "He'll give you a right ticking off."

I really didn't care what they said to Da because I never saw him. The first morning in Saltcoats, I asked where he was and was he coming to the beach with us. "He went out" I was told. And when he came back in the middle of the afternoon I knew where he'd been. At that time, pubs opened from 11am to 2.30 pm, and then from 5 to 10 pm. And that's where he spent his holidays, apart from taking a 'siesta', as he called it, in the hut in the afternoon.

When we first went to the beach Mr. Nolan spread his arms to the sea and said; "Isn't it great to get away from it all!" But for Da, 'getting away from it all' meant not just escaping from his monotonous job, but also getting away from us. And that's why he wasn't there to save me. Holidays for Da meant drinking, betting, reading the paper and blethering with whoever sat next to him in the pub. His wife and children were bound up in his mind with the world of work. He worked to pay for our food and lodgings, but when he didn't have to work, we didn't exist. So I didn't care what they said to him about what happened at the beach. I knew it would just become a pub story for him to tell the next day to anyone who was half-listening. "You know, the sea can be really dangerous. My wee boy had the fright of his life the other day. He went swimming..."

These few days at resorts on the windswept coasts of Ayrshire and East Lothian were the only holidays I spent with my family. We never travelled anywhere else in Scotland, not even to Edinburgh, which was less than an hour by train. My own country was a foreign land. I heard about places like Aberdeen and Falkirk and Kilmarnock, but for me they were just the names of football teams. They were as unknown to me as Vladivostok. London was a place that only existed in the BBC news. Even the smart

West End of Glasgow and Kelvinside were as distant as the moon, although they were only a bus ride away. We were locked in our little enclave. We only made short journeys to Woolworths, Celtic park, Aunt Peggy's, or the swimming baths. I can't explain our narrow existence. In his Navy days Da had sailed down the West African coast. When he was with us, he could only sail into the nearest pub. The result was that we were sailing away from each other.

So, the rest of my school holidays meant weeks of hanging around Easterhouse with my mates, and we were simply left to fend for ourselves except for Duffy. His parents took him away for weeks at a time, and once he even went to stay with an aunt in London. When he returned we treated him like an adventurer who had discovered the source of the Nile. And then Frank Thompson boasted that he was going to Spain on a plane! When he returned, we were amazed by his suntan and the souvenirs he brought back: ornaments of Spanish bulls, castanets and coloured fans. He'd had dinner at 10 pm. - not his tea at 5. It all sounded so exotic and unbelievable.

The rest of us were stuck on the housing estate, but we had the country walks and the lochs, which saved us from the monotony of the scheme. And during the holidays, with no school bells to interrupt our games, they started and finished whenever we wanted. Our long trips to the lochs had no time constraints: only our rumbling stomachs drove us home. Normal bed times and getting up times were not imposed. Long chapters of books could be finished, and then another started. A request to watch

TV late in the evening would be granted if I was careful to ask while massaging Ma's sore back.

I often found myself alone in the flat during the day. I dribbled my football all around it, avoiding Da's foul-smelling room, and scored a million goals against the front door. I bounced from one bed to another, from chair to sofa then leapt like Spiderman to grab the windowsill and I did handstands against the walls. I loved to shadow-box. I would put on my red plastic boxing gloves and skip and hop around, knocking out heavyweights right, left and centre. I played skittles in the hall, placing them against the front door and bowling as hard as I could, making a terrific racket. Noisier still were the live concerts to a hundred thousand adoring fans. I would put a heavy rock LP on my brother's record player, take up my tennis racket and play complex riffs. Inexplicably, Mrs Lynch didn't appreciate my sell-out concerts and would put an end to them by banging her broom handle on her ceiling. With no pressure from others, I put pressure on myself by setting all kinds of challenges such as aiming to read a certain number of books every week. In that time-less state, I was probably much more active than when I was at school.

Christmas was a special holiday. At school and at church we learned hymns and carols and there were re-hearsals for the Nativity Play. Throughout December we were caught up in a Christmas mood. The 8th of December was the date of 'The Immaculate Conception', which had a magical ring to it. We had to practice the hymns a lot in order to learn the Latin words by heart. Apart from the first line, which our teacher or the priest would translate, we hadn't a clue what we were singing about as we chanted '*Venite Adoremus Dominum*' in our East End Glasgow accent. It sounded pretty good to us, and made us feel part of the chosen faithful since it was in a foreign language, which our Protestant pals couldn't match. I liked the long '*Gloria in Excelsis Deo*'. To my pals and me it was like a football chant to God. Some of the hymns were in English, but that made them less mysterious, and soppier. I had to admit the Catholic Church had some catchy tunes. I hummed hymns and carols up and down our stairs, playing with the echo effect of the Close.

Christmas was also about giving and receiving presents, of course. I always gave Da a pair of socks or a handkerchief with the initial 'J' in the corner, and a box of After Eights to Ma. Santa Claus was pretty good to me, as he usually brought me at least half the things I asked for in the letter which I sent up the chimney. I particularly remember an Action Man, a Scalextric racing track, an electric train set and a Robin Hood outfit complete with bow and arrow. The picture on the Scalextric box looked fabulous with its red Ferraris, but when I tried to set up the plastic track in our living room it looked less attractive. The electric connections were never perfectly joined together, so the cars would stall and fall off. It was the same with the train set. Nothing ever worked. So I ended up pushing the electric train with its shaky plastic wagons round the plastic lines until I got fed up and picked up Oor Wullie or The Broons instead.

The year I got my Robin Hood outfit was also the year

that Santa died. I discovered the box containing the costume in the hall cupboard a couple of days before Christmas, before I had sent my letter up the chimney. I had half expected that he didn't exist, but didn't want to acknowledge it for fear of not getting any presents. On Christmas day I feigned surprise and dressed up in my green outfit with its snazzy green hat and fired my rubber-tipped arrow at the Sheriff of Nottingham. My presents were not from the North Pole. They were from Woolworths in Parkhead. Some of the magic had gone out of Christmas.

But it was still special. There was the hallowed atmosphere of midnight mass in a crowded church, with the smell of incense in the air. There was the tang of tangerines and the spicy fruitiness of mince pies. And then there was our mantlepiece, decked with cards covered in glitter with images of the Virgin gazing at her rosy-cheeked baby. And on TV, we were captivated by the cartoon version of *A Christmas Carol*.

Hogmanay was magical too, with Uncle Jerry, Auntie Kathleen, Grandma and some of the neighbours. They would all take turns to sing, even my Ma and Da. He often sang about preferring to be in love than to be a millionaire, which I doubted, and Ma sang the Judy Garland song *Somewhere Over the Rainbow*. I understood her choice. Jerry and Kathleen were the best singers. Jerry closed his eyes and sang the Blues as if he were the saddest man in the world. Kathleen would sing standing up with a cigarette in one hand and a glass of sherry in the other. Her head would sway as she sang *Hello Dolly* or *My Love is like a Red Red Rose* in her wavering soprano. It was strange when the bells rang at midnight. It was the only time of the year that we actually touched each other. We had to stand up and hug one another and say "Happy New Year!" Kathleen and Jerry did it with true feeling, but the rest of us were pretty awkward and gave quick embarrassed hugs. Singing *Auld Land Syne* was like the final toll of the church bell. It signalled the end of my evening as I was then sent to bed before the serious drinking started. It also meant the end of the year, and the end of the holidays.

"Holidays are jolly days!" said Billy Bunter, one of my favourite characters, on the eve of his mid-term break. "Jolly jolly holidays!" They were something I looked forward to and I was sad when they ended. Like singing *Auld Lang Syne,* holidays made me feel both jolly and melancholy. They were periods which would end, leaving a new and uncertain future which I wanted to put off as long as possible. After the holidays all my classmates looked different, even after the short Christmas break. I felt I was different, too. Holidays punctuated our childhood, and made us aware that we were growing up.

14. THE LIBRARY

There was a life-changing moment during my childhood when I realised that I could read the words on a page. This was a magical discovery. But I was perplexed by the contrast between the words spoken by my family, friends and neighbours, and the words that I read in books. Real people uttered predictable things like 'Right then, it's time you left for school' and 'This will do you good!' which was always said before we were given castor oil. Words used by the adults in my life were hard and direct, sometimes coarse and vulgar, and were usually orders and prohibitions. Or they were hackneyed phrases and expressions, churned out as if they were universal truths like 'Children should be seen, not heard'. In the world of books it was different. In books, words were interesting and enchanting, mysteriously evoking all kinds of strange worlds. They sounded melodious when read aloud. Words could unveil the complexity of life and stimulate the mind.

My brother noticed that I could read and that I was captivated by whatever I laid my hands on, which was usually the Beano. He told me that comics were all very well, but I should join the library and read real books as well.

This wasn't as easy as it sounded. Having built a housing scheme for 50,000 people, the Council must have run out of money or ideas. There was no gym, swimming pool, theatre or cinema. And there was clearly no need for a library. What did the residents need books for when they couldn't even read the signs telling them not to drop litter?

So I had to take the bus to the tiny library in the neighbouring town of Garthamlock. My brother came with me the first time to show me around and to get a membership card; after that I went alone. Garthamlock library didn't look the way I had imagined a library would be. It was a small, squat, intimidating building with wire mesh covering the windows, and it was surrounded by a barbed-wire fence on top of a concrete wall. It looked more like a store for dangerous chemicals than a library.

When I dared to open the door, I was struck by the strange hush which loomed over the place. This made the atmosphere as dead and gloomy as the church. There were a few elderly people browsing the bookshelves aimlessly. The librarian was a thin, sad-looking, bespectacled man with hair sticking out of his ears and nose. He took the form which my parents had signed, studied it carefully, then wrote my name and address on three red tickets which he solemnly presented to me. I looked at them with joy and pride as if I had been given a pass to a new world. Then he pointed me towards the junior section, which was deserted. I could choose three books and keep them for up to a fortnight, but I had to bring them back in perfect condition, before a date which he would stamp on each book. He emphasised the word 'borrowed'. He threatened in a whisper that if I returned them late, or didn't bring them back at all, my parents would be made to pay a fine or even the cost of replacing the books. I would be banned for life from every library in the City of Glasgow. He glowered at me to show he meant business, and I nodded to show I understood the gravity of bringing *Winnie the Pooh* back a day late. Then he put his finger to his lips to indicate strict silence. And with that he left me alone. Another advocate of the 'children should be seen, not heard' school.

But I had a problem staying silent for very long. I had a terrible cough. In fact, I spent long periods of my childhood spluttering through coughing fits. Maybe it was because of the wet weather and the permanent dampness. Ma would give me revolting cough syrup which smelled like gasoline, but it had no effect at all. It just made me gasp for water to wash away the oil-slick in my mouth. I was also given acidic cough drops which made my eyes stream. Unfortunately, I was in a coughing phase on my first library visit. The librarian lifted his head from his book and glared at me. I put my hand to my mouth to control my rebellious throat but could feel it was about to erupt. I spluttered out a machine-gun cough and my eyes watered. Suddenly the librarian was standing behind me, keeping his distance as if I were a leper. He hissed, "Germs and books don't go together. This is not a hospital. This is a library. A *public* library. So don't spread your germs here." I spluttered back, "I've chosen my books anyway. I was just leaving." And then I grabbed the three nearest books, had them stamped, and left.

And that was the luck of the draw. My first obsessive reading craze began. The books came from the section *Tales from Foreign Lands.* I had *Russian Folk Tales, Tales from the German Forests* and *Tales from the Far East.* I had a fortnight to read them but I finished them in a week.

During subsequent visits I only chose books with the word 'Tales' on the cover because I knew that I would like them as they would have absolutely nothing to do with my world. Yet I always felt a connection with the heroic characters, particularly the small boys facing incredible ordeals involving vicious animals, wicked witches and evil warlords. There were ogres and trolls everywhere, not just in Glasgow. This was comforting.

After reading *The Arabian Nights*, I had a hankering for something exciting and different, but closer to my own world. So I started to read the collections which filled half the fiction shelves in the junior library. They were easy to spot as each had its own colour. The pink and green rows were the Enid Blyton series. I couldn't wait to get started, and began with her.

But that was a mistake. I was very soon bored out of my mind, despite my willingness to give anything a try. All the *Famous Five* and *Secret Seven* 'characters' were as hollow to me as *Noddy*, her other wooden creation. The prose was lifeless and uninspiring, the stories seemed like nonsense, and they were terribly dull compared to the fantastic worlds conjured up in the books of tales.

I discovered other books which were just as implausible, but they were funny and certainly much livelier.

The *Billy Bunter* books occupied a whole shelf. They were fat and yellow rather like the character himself, and I set myself the goal of reading them all. I took out three episodes of the saga of 'The Fat Owl of Greyfriars' every time I went to the library over the following weeks. I liked the fact that he embodied everything that we were not supposed to do. He was a grotesquely fat, myopic, slothful glutton, constantly complaining about his lot, surrounded by decent chaps like Harry Wharton, the school captain. Bunter was thick-headed and deceitful, begging his companions to lend him money which he would pay back when he received a postal order, which never arrived, from his parents, who also never visited. Almost every book began in the same way: '"Yarooh!" went the Fat Owl of the Remove...' as Bunter found himself embroiled in yet another mess. I read them as fast as I could turn the pages. Every book was 256 pages long. That always amazed me, as if Bunter's adventures suddenly stopped like a train arriving at a station on time. One day, when I took back my three Bunter books after only a week, the librarian asked me if I didn't like them and did I want to try something else? I said that I thought they were very good. Then he asked me if I had actually read them, and I told him I had read all three. He said I was fibbing, so I recounted the three wild plots before he handed back my three red tickets. I took out three more, thumping them defiantly on the desk for him to stamp. "Goodbye" I said, and added, "See you next week." After that, he didn't ask me again if I had read the books.

I had enjoyed reading about the disobedient characters

in my comics, and now I was attracted to and repelled by Billy Bunter's many vices. I was delighted by the humour in these stories.

I also loved the *William* stories by Richmal Crompton. Unlike Billy Bunter, William was a character I identified with; he was a scruffily-dressed eleven year old, always up to pranks and getting into fights. I liked the titles - they guided my reading progress. Starting with *Just William,* I read them all; *More William, William Again* and so on. Whenever I put them on the counter to be stamped, I wondered if the librarian would censor them. There was a joyful naughtiness in these books which I found exciting. It offered some relief from the relentless saintliness which I was supposed to aspire to as a Catholic.

I enjoyed the *Jennings* series about a mischievous schoolboy at a swish English public school. My head became cluttered with the posh schoolboy slang used by Jennings and his pals. Miss Savage would smile whenever I uttered expressions like 'Oh crumbs!', and 'Jolly good, old chum' in my Glasgow accent.

But before long I abandoned the cosy world of school life for tales of adventure. That's when I discovered the *Biggles* books. Biggles was an ace pilot, who fought in the First War, but somehow managed to remain young enough to fight in the Second War then carry out secret missions during the Cold War. I imagined myself jumping into the cockpit and battling ferocious enemy forces. That was during my Airfix phase. My life was simply Biggles and Airfix, every day for weeks on end.

I decided that Biggles was too 'stiff upper lip' for my

liking, and I fell for *Horatio Hornblower*. This was a series about the British Navy, set during the Napoleonic Wars. Midshipman Hornblower faced enormous challenges: storms, battles, shipwrecks. Unlike Biggles, he often experienced failure, leading to pages of self-doubt and uncertainty. He was an endearing character who never fully realised how admired he was for his bravery, intelligence, and dignity.

Then at last the Council decided to build a library in an effort to combat the growing gang warfare in Easterhouse. It was a pre-fabricated building, quickly set up and filled with books, which gang members were encouraged to dip into instead of slashing each other. I became a member, but I doubt if many of the gang members joined; I never saw one.

I was obsessed by finishing the book I had started. I devoured the pages as I went along. That was the great thing about collections like the *William* books or *Hornblower*. I knew the context, setting, the minor characters and the protagonist. So I flew through such books, becoming totally absorbed by the plot. Then I'd start a new one, and become lost again in a fictional world.

From the age of ten I began to keep notebooks in which I recorded all the books I had read. I wanted their contents to mirror the shelves at the library. I was never a browser. I was obsessed with a character or an author. So when I read the whole shelf of Billy Bunter books I meticulously noted down each title, and it felt as if they were mine in some way. Other obsessions followed. At twelve, I became fascinated by Rider Haggard and read everything he wrote. Then followed P.C. Wren, Jules Verne, Alexandre Dumas and Arthur Conan Doyle.

In the library I was surrounded by books, whereas at home I only had my comics. It never occurred to me to buy a book, and no one ever gave me one as a present. The only book I was given was a prize for coming first in class in my final year at Primary school. I remember smelling and touching the brand new book; it was spotlessly clean, so unlike the grubby books in the library. It was called *The Day of the Dingo*. At first I was afraid to turn its crisp pages, but finally I set to it. It was awful; insipid, dull and in the Enid Blyton tradition. Having tasted Dumas, Dickens, and Conan Doyle, it seemed like a book for eight year olds. I placed it beside my brother's books in our room. He had quite a lot of books, but I was forbidden from reading them. He said I had to wait until I was older, because they were too 'difficult' for me. I vaguely understood that to mean they were stories about relationships between women and men. Women only existed in my books as mothers, sisters or glamorous heroines.

At the age of eleven, the librarian allowed me to 'peruse the works' in the adult section. There I discovered non-fiction, and in particular a fabulous series produced by Time Life Publications. These were large books with glossy pages full of incredible photos, charts and illustrations. So, armed with my three tickets I started to select a non-fiction book alongside two works of fiction. The Time Life books were mind-expanding; they opened my eyes to the world, and to past civilisations. The next day at school I would find a pretext to show off my vast knowledge of whatever I had studied.

One day the teacher told Hogie to stop 'monkeying about'. Later, in the playground, Hogie bounced up and down inspecting Mintsy's hair for lice, and Duffy declared that "Hogie is proof that we are descended from monkeys."

"I'm a monkey! I'm a gorilla!" Hogie snarled, cock-eyed and bent-kneed.

"Gorillas aren't monkeys" I sniffed, knowingly, "Gorillas are Apes."

"What's the difference?" Mintsy enquired. And that was my cue to share the knowledge recently acquired from my Time Life book. "Gorillas, chimpanzees, and orang-utans don't have tails. By the way, orang-utan means 'man of the forest'. Monkeys, on the other hand, are usually much smaller and have tails to keep their balance as they run along branches."

Everyone acknowledged my great wisdom with silent respect.

And I concluded: "But Hogie is a rare example. He is both an ape and a monkey!" And the screeching, scratching and chest pounding began again.

I had become the world's biggest bore on primates. I wanted information, I needed facts, and I found my facts in books.

So both these grim libraries became my own private places of worship. And unlike prayers in church, my prayers here were answered. I was entertained, informed and stimulated. Jack London's *White Fang* and *The Call of the Wild* summed up my childhood joy of reading. I could identify with a wolf surviving in a hostile environment.

Books were my route out of Glasgow into different worlds. They gave me the confidence and inspiration to try to find something, somewhere, which might become my Treasure Island.

15. PAPER ROUND

Later in my childhood I sorely needed more money, to fund my ever-expanding interests, one of which was music. I was desperate to acquire LPs by rock groups like Deep Purple and Grand Funk Railroad. I also wanted to go to 'the pictures' to see all the new films like *Easy Rider,* and to buy some special items of clothing which Ma would never have agreed to buy, like the red 'Che Lives' T-shirt which I coveted. My pocket money was inadequate, and being 'a good Catholic', it never occurred to me to shoplift as some classmates did. I had to earn some money, so I had to work. I was in good company; Charles Dickens had been twelve when he began working at the blacking factory.

Then a pal called Gerald Doherty told me that his big brother, Willie, was going to give up his paper round, as he was starting an apprenticeship. Newspaper delivery rounds were hard to get, and only changed hands if you knew the kid who was giving one up, and you could offer them some compensation. I met Willie the next day, prepared to flatter him, but this wasn't necessary, as he declared "any friend of Gerald is a friend of mine". With this new and special bond between us, he gave me the paper round, on the understanding that I would give him my takings from my first Sunday in the job. Of course I agreed, delighted to have found a source of income. Working for nothing for the first Sunday was a small price to pay for such a job. He gave me a little red book with all the names and addresses of his customers and the different newspapers they subscribed to. He told me to collect payment for the papers on the preceding Friday. "If you don't", he warned, "you won't get paid". He said he would tell the 'paper man' that I was his replacement, and he advised me to go and see him to introduce myself.

So off I went to see the 'paper man'. I found him in a dump of a place in Swinton, between Easterhouse and Baillieston, a good half hour's walk from our flat. A boy around my age pointed him out to me, and whispered "He's called Tam". I approached him and said "Hello" and in return received a stare that said 'Who is this insect?' "I'm taking over Willie's round." I continued. "Is that so?" he replied, "We'll see about that."

Although he was probably only in his early twenties, his unkempt hair, dirty clothes and unshaven face made him seem much older. He looked like a Dickensian character, with his shifty eyes and scowl, and when he spoke, he snarled like a dog. The amount he paid us for distributing the newspapers was ridiculously low. The only reason anyone accepted the job (which he knew full well) was because of the tips they hoped to receive. But the risk, as all the paper boys told me, was that one might have too many mean customers. If you had a good round, you could make two or three pounds in tips, with a bonus at Christmas.

Tam didn't ask my name. He just wanted to check that I understood that I was to pay him for the newspapers he gave me - the full amount, in cash, on Sunday morning. If anyone didn't pay me, that was my problem, and I would have to pay him out of my own pocket. I nodded, but wondered if I was making the right decision.

"Be here on Sunday morning at 6.15 sharp. No later."

I checked out the streets and the names and addresses of my customers. I was worried as the round included Aberdalgie Road which was unfamiliar territory. I kept a low profile, hoping nobody would notice me, particularly the teenage thugs who picked on strangers in their area. Next, I had to find a wheelbarrow to carry my papers as Willie had given his away. Fortunately, I spotted an old set of pram wheels on a rubbish tip. I got a sturdy old wooden crate from the grocer's and with a few nails and wire my Da gave me, I managed to attach the crate to the wheels. Then I hammered on two poles as handlebars. It looked terrible, but the upside was I could leave it anywhere; nobody would bother to steal it.

My first contact with customers was a disaster. I set off to collect the money on the Friday. I got no answer at the first door I knocked on. After banging a few more times, a young child eventually opened the door slightly, and peeked out. Trying to be as pleasant as possible, I told the kid to get his Mammy as I was the new paper boy, come to collect the paper money. "Don't know you" he said, and shut the door in my face. This happened at door after door. Sometimes if I was lucky, an older brother or sister or even a parent would appear. Some paid reluctantly, but only after lengthy explanations on my part. There was never a tip. But a number of them refused to pay, suspicious that I was trying it on.

Getting money out of my Glaswegian neighbours on a Friday night was no easy task. Like the insurance man or the HP collectors, I didn't give them anything right there and then, so they were reluctant to pay for the service. In the beginning they didn't recognise my knock, so I had to develop my own style, distinct from that of the milkman and the insurance man. I also realised that I had to appear at the same time every week to get the door to open. On that first Friday it struck me that each household went silent after I knocked. I put my ear to the door and it seemed that everyone had frozen, as if the police were on their doorstep. I would knock again and if the door finally opened, the usual tactic was that the youngest child would be sent to see who was there. The kid would have strict instructions to say that his parents weren't in, unless it was a 'friendly' caller. I had to become a friendly caller.

So I was in a situation where I would have to pay Tam with my own money, then pay Willie the tips I hadn't even managed to collect. I wasn't making any money, in fact I was about to lose a lot of money. I was wasting my time knocking on doors which mostly didn't open. I had to revise my business plan.

I decided to abandon all efforts to raise the money, and went to see Willie to beg him to accompany me, to re-

assure his former customers. He finally agreed, as he realised he wouldn't get any money either if he didn't vouch
for me. So all through Saturday we knocked on doors and
I managed to get most of the money with only a few exceptions. Willie told me this was normal. And if families
continued to avoid paying, I had to inform Tam.

At last my first money-making scheme was under way.

The first few rounds took twice as long as the subsequent ones as I had to get used to where to go, who was
who, and which papers to give them. But soon I got the
hang of my wheelbarrow and the route round my customers, and I began to deliver the papers much more
quickly. Getting up at 5.30 on Sunday was less easy to
get used to. There was no one about at that ungodly
hour. I was up even before the priest for early mass. The
only noise as I trundled through the streets was the grating squeal and rattle of my wheelbarrow. My customers
indulged in the ritual of reading the Sunday papers in
bed or over breakfast. A lot of people didn't read papers
during the week, but would never dream of missing their
Sunday paper with its special features and colour maga-
zines. Sunday wouldn't be Sunday without a newspaper.
I was taking an active part in a ritual. Like the priest during mass, giving out the Eucharist and the word of God to
the faithful, I was giving out the word of the Press. But I
reckoned that I was more popular than the priest.

So while the rest of the world slept, I went to the paper
hut, counted my papers, paid Tam, and set off. I had over
400 papers to deliver. The most popular was *The Sunday
Post*, closely followed by *The Sunday Mail*. Then there was

the lurid *News of the World* with its sensational headlines of celebrity sex scandals. A few families subscribed to the 'quality press', *The Sunday Times* and *The Sunday Observer*, which were very heavy, so I was thankful that they were in the minority.

The delivery was a real physical effort as I had to push my wheelbarrow from the hut in Swinton all the way up Aberdalgie Road. And 400 papers weigh a ton. It was exhausting pushing the barrow up the slope on Easterhouse Road at the beginning of the round when I had a full load. I had to race up the stairs with a dozen papers, all sorted out in correct order and then rush back down, glancing out of every landing window to check that nobody was pinching my papers. My clattering on the stairs set the dogs barking, and some of them breakfasted on *The Sunday Mail* as I rammed it through the letterbox. When I reached a customer who was a bad payer, I would tug the paper back and forth in the letterbox to make the dogs wild with excitement. I would feel them tearing the other end to pieces. Some customers gave me good tips, so I slipped their paper silently through their letterbox, making sure it shut quietly. Those who gave me nothing would hear their letter box rattle a few times after the paper had been pushed through.

The worst days were when it rained heavily all morning, which was not unusual. That added an extra hour to the paper round as I had to keep slipping the plastic cover on and off the wheelbarrow to try to keep the papers dry. If it was also windy, then it really was hell. My plastic cover would blow all over the place and the papers and I would all get soaked.

There is a scene in Ken Loach's *Kes*, in which the main character, Billy, is on his paper round. He has a few cheeky words with the milkman as he passes, and while the milkman attends to his deliveries, Billy swipes a bottle of milk and drinks it later, while he reads *Desperate Dan*. I have to confess that I regularly did the same thing except that I took a bottle from a doorstep, and always from a different one. I convinced myself that this was redistribution of wealth from the rich to the poor - I was Robin Hood. The 'rich' were the deluded customers who were rude and self important, the misers who never gave tips, and the unscrupulous who hadn't paid. I was the 'poor', and towards the end of my round I would allocate myself a short break, and taking a bottle of milk from one of the 'rich' customers I would sit in a quiet Close, drink the milk, and read the headlines. And if there had been no milk for my cornflakes that morning, I thought my actions justifiable.

As time went by I had no difficulty getting paid by the majority of families and soon I was earning my much hoped-for tips. But there were a dozen or so families where there was always a big fuss, and I had to return again and again to get the money. These families were experts in dealing with debt-collectors, the insurance man, and even the police. I was last on their list of creditors to be paid. The door often remained shut no matter how many times I knocked and hammered. If the door did open, and the youngest child said, "my ma's not in," I would put my foot in the door and try to push it a little more, but there was always an older brother on the other side, keeping it firmly in place. They knew all the tricks.

There were two families I really disliked as they had decided that attack was the best form of defence. The men would open the door with an air of outrage, denying that I had delivered the papers the previous week. They would threaten to call the police. I should be ashamed of myself for trying to cheat poor hard-working families. The only solution with these people was sheer force. If they didn't pay three times in a row Tam sent round a 'heavy' to 'lean on' them. Then they would always pay me the following Friday. But they were playing one creditor off against another, so after a fortnight the same thing would happen again.

One positive aspect of the job was that my mathematical skills developed. My teacher couldn't believe how well I answered any arithmetic question. She didn't know that every Friday I had to quickly work out accurately what everybody owed me. Those who had fallen behind on their payments were increasingly unwilling to pay their arrears and they were always looking for ways to cheat me. In those days, of course, we used the imperial system: pounds, shillings and pence. And there were so many coins; pennies, shillings, florins, half-crowns and so on. Doing calculations on the basis of 12 and 20, and adding up in this archaic system meant that I had to think fast to avoid being fleeced by my customers.

The paper round gave me an education which was very different from the one I got at school. Many of the toddlers who came to the door were filthy and smelly. Some wore only a dirty vest. I hated it when one of the men or women were drunk, and would insist that I come inside to be paid. It seemed to me that their flats were not homes. There was torn linoleum on the floor, the kitchen was a mess of unwashed dishes, and pans of fish fingers or sausages burned on the stove. The living room was dominated by the TV, and in front of it would be a large battered armchair for the man of the house. A sofa was home to various cats and dogs. The wallpaper was ghastly and the lighting a gruesome yellow. There was no comfort here.

Although I was still young, I quickly gained a good understanding of the hierarchies within the working class. My Da was a turner and my Ma was a part-time cleaner. They had no property or savings, but they had steady jobs. They could pay the rent and feed and clothe us more or less adequately. On the paper round I saw families like ours which were managing to get by, but also saw many others who had much less than us. The men either did labouring jobs on an irregular basis, or were unemployed. And then there were the families with real social problems. The paper round gave me a glimpse of lives made squalid by alcoholism and violence. These adults seemed hopeless and helpless. They laughed stupidly like kids and couldn't utter a sentence without swearing. Some of them tried to bully me because I was a child. I didn't feel any pity for them, but I did feel sorry for their 'weans'. They were the real victims. Were they condemned to be like their lousy parents?

At the end of the round I trundled my empty barrow back home, looking forward to my Sunday breakfast of bacon, eggs and potato scones which I demolished while reading the newspaper. My brother had insisted that we subscribe to *The Sunday Times*, a 'quality' newspaper. It reported on events happening around the world, which made an impression during that strange transition between childhood and adolescence. It was there that I read about the death of Che Guevara in 1967. I was instantly attracted to the myth that surrounded the revolutionary leader. With the earnings from my paper round, I not only bought my LPs, but also the much coveted 'Che Lives' T-shirt. I wore it to school under my uniform. I was like Clark Kent. I felt secretly empowered as I sat meekly at my desk.

Once, in French class, 'Che' got me into trouble. It was our first year of French and we had a horrible teacher called Mr Devlin who obviously hated his job, and clearly detested us. He was huge, with a big black beard and heavy-lidded eyes. Nobody listened to what he said and nobody learned anything. He would write sentences in French on the blackboard and we had to copy them, but we hadn't a clue what they meant. One day I felt his creepy presence behind my back as we were copying from the blackboard. He snatched my jotter and held it up as if it were a dirty rag, saying "What's this?" On the back of my jotter in gigantic capital letters in red ink, was written *CHE LIVES*. Mr Devlin wasn't amused.

"What's that supposed to mean?"

"Nothing, sir."

"What do you mean 'nothing'? This is a political statement, boy!"

"It's just my jotter, sir, the back of my jotter. I didn't write on the desk."

"Your jotter is public property. Your jotter is for your schoolwork. This is graffiti written on public property. Political graffiti."

I wanted to rip off my uniform and expose my 'Che Lives' T-shirt but Mr Devlin's furious features dissuaded me. Instead, he tore off the back of my jotter and threw it in the bin. Then he gave me four strokes of the belt, and told me to keep politics out of the classroom. That evening I put Joan Baez on the record-player singing, 'We shall overcome...' I hummed along, proud to have been belted for Che.

And all of this was because of the articles I had read in *The Sunday Times*. Now I saw the Sunday newspapers differently. They weren't just bringing sex and trivia, some of them were bringing the real 'news of the world'. I had read a news story and formed an opinion. As Mr Devlin had said, I had made 'a political statement'.

The next morning, still wearing my 'Che Lives' T-shirt under my white shirt, I looked in the mirror, trying to copy Che's determined look. I thought to myself, "Watch out! Jim lives!" I only wished I had a beret and a Cuban cigar.

16. AE FOND KISS

It was towards the end of my final year at primary
school, and I was eleven, going on twelve. I was daydream-
ing in class, gazing at the floor. Suddenly I started, as if
someone had seized me by the throat. My eyes had focused on something which shook me to the core. It was
a pair of legs. They were crossed and I could see part of
a thigh under a pleated skirt. I looked up and saw Mary
Timothy sitting immobile at her desk. Mary was not in
the same league as my idol, Ann Bolan, the class beauty,
who never deigned to speak to any of the boys. Mary was
plain and no one noticed her. No one, except me. My eyes
fell upon her legs again. They were bewitching. I just
couldn't take my eyes off them. Suddenly, I realised that
Mintsy was looking at me curiously. He turned to look in
the direction of my gaze. I looked up at the ceiling, sticking my pen in my mouth like a poet seeking inspiration
from the muses. When I could no longer resist turning
my gaze back to Mary's legs, they had moved. She had un-
crossed her legs and sat with both feet firmly planted on
the floor. No thigh now, just skirt.

I looked at Miss Savage and pretended to be interested
in what she was saying. A lightning bolt struck a sec-

ond time; she also had attractive legs! I had never noticed them before. I couldn't stop staring. Then the bell rang shattering my daydream. I got up feeling strangely guilty. Mary Timothy put on her coat and became her usual plain self again, in her brown skirt and pigtails. Miss Savage stood up and let us out for the afternoon break. Something had happened, which I did not understand. Something was stirring in me, something new and uncontrollable. Outside in the playground I joined a game of football and kicked the ball as hard as I could. I focused on the goalposts rather than Mary's legs, and scored twice, briefly becoming my old self again.

But at the weekend it was clear that legs had become my new obsession. At that time there was a TV variety show called *Sunday Night at the London Palladium*. It featured comedians like Ken Dodd, and pop groups like the Beatles and Gerry and the Pacemakers. The show always began with 'The Chorus Girls', a group of about twenty women wearing tight-fitting sparkly tops, tights and ostrich feathers in their hair. I had always thought they were ludicrous, with their beaming smiles, as they kicked their legs in the air and moved arm in arm around the stage. But now I found them fascinating. I was no longer interested in Ken Dodd. My eyes were glued to the TV, watching the dancing girls showing off those fabulous long legs. The same thing happened with *Top of the Pops*. I had barely noticed 'Pan's People' before, but now I was riveted. Suddenly, I wanted to dance, and to see girls dancing.

My prayers were about to be answered. The gym teacher,

Mr Bailey, told us that we needed 'polishing'. I imagined that he was going to pour Johnson's wax over us, but by 'polishing' he meant that we were going to learn what he called 'social skills'. We were going to learn to dance 'properly'. So he lined up the girls on one side of the assembly hall, and the boys on the other.

Our first dance was 'The Gay Gordons'. Mr Bailey chose the tallest girl, Patricia Murphy, and led her through the movements a few times while sounding out the beat: "One and two and three and...turn." We could barely contain ourselves. We found Mr Bailey's prancing steps quite ridiculous, but we managed to stifle our giggles. Next, he put on a record and told us that when we heard the dramatic introductory chord, the boys had to choose their partners. The chord sounded, but nobody moved. Nobody was going to be as ludicrous as Mr. Bailey. He blew his top, and threatened us with the belt if we "didn't play the game". Mr Bailey added that if any boy was left without a partner the next time, he would have the pleasure of dancing with him - after being belted. We got the message and we were under starter's orders. I set my sights on Ann Bolan, as did all of my classmates. The chord struck and we all flew at the good-looking girls. Tom McFadyen, who was bigger than the rest of us, got to Ann first. We all tried to push him out of the way, but he held on to his prize. Mr Bailey blew his whistle, and shouted "you're not playing rugby!" and ordered us all back to our places to start again.

I decided to change my strategy, and give up all hope of obtaining Ann Bolan's hand - at least for the moment. I focused on Philomena O'Hannigan. I liked her name. She was small, dark-haired with nice brown eyes and an olive complexion, which was unusual in Glasgow. At that time, I simply divided girls into two categories: good-looking or not. Character didn't interest me. There were girls I never looked at: the majority, I suppose. And there were a few whom I wanted to be close to. There was something about the hair and complexion of these girls, and the shape of their mouths which pleased me. But something new was happening. Now I wanted to touch them. Dancing was the perfect opportunity. I was delighted at Mr Bailey's decision to 'polish' me.

My strategy worked. I found my partner; Philomena accepted my invitation. I was thrilled. I took her hand awkwardly in mine. We didn't speak or look at one another. Then the opening chord struck, and we moved forward to the marching melody of the 'The Gay Gordons'. I felt that I was marching into a new life. Philomena kept the beat perfectly and guided me at every turn. This was a delicious new pleasure. I was holding a girl's hand and waist for the first time in my life. Boys suddenly seemed less interesting, and my pals, like Hogie, looked like grinning louts. I liked Philomena's serious face. Her fingers were fine and delicate and spotlessly clean - unlike mine. Her hair smelled wonderful, like the perfume counter at *Boots*. I was intoxicated by its clean sweetness. I vowed to have a soapy bath that night and scrub my hair till it shone like the Brylcream advert. But the music stopped, and without saying a word, Philomena walked away to join the other girls and I drifted back to the boys' wall.

Mr Bailey made us change partners for the other dances. I found myself in the scramble for partners with some of the girls whose names I hardly knew. But I liked having my arm around their waist, and holding their soft clean hands. And I saw them all with new eyes from then on. They were no longer just faceless girls in the class. Suddenly they were appealing in their own way, and I realised that Ann Bolan was not the only girl worth looking at. I had a whole class full of girls around me.

Another significant development took place at church. A new priest arrived at St Clare's to help "to spread the Word of the Lord in the Parish" as he put it, adding "particularly to the young". He stared at the front rows where we, 'the young', were sitting at mass, wondering what was in store for us. The new priest was called Father Doyle. He was tall and thin and much younger than our two parish priests. He looked in our direction and smiled benevolently - something we'd never seen a priest do before. We were very wary. Then he did something astonishing. He pulled out a guitar and started strumming it - in church! We couldn't believe it. He started singing a joyful song in praise of Jesus. Father Kelly looked on in stony silence and we followed his example. When Father Doyle finished, we wondered if we should applaud. Father Kelly gave us no sign to do so, and carried on with mass with an air of disapproval. We lowered our eyes and put on our pious faces. At the end of the mass, Father Doyle made an announcement. He said he was organising a disco on Friday nights. Instead of "roaming the streets at the mercy of gangs" we would come together in the church hall to listen to music and be happy. It sounded too good to be true.

Father Doyle was a 'swinging' priest who believed that God was a bit fed-up with solemn Latin hymns. He told us the Church was changing and that there were many ways to God, and that electric guitars was one of them. Apparently, God liked Jimi Hendrix, and even Mick Jagger. Then we heard, to our immense joy, that the first Friday night Church Disco would be a real one with flashing lights and our favourite music blaring out of two big loudspeakers. It was simply incredible!

Friday came and the girls were no longer in their dull brown and yellow uniforms. They were wearing brightly coloured short skirts and blouses. They were even wearing make-up, and some were wearing platform shoes which made them seem remarkably tall. The girls were dancing in the centre of the floor. Father Doyle was overseeing the proceedings with a satisfied smile, while nodding to the beat. We praised the Lord for sending us this messenger, who was performing miracles.

There were different rules at the Church Disco compared to Mr Bailey's highland dances. We watched a couple of older boys to learn the ropes. They went up to two girls and tapped them on the shoulder. The girls turned to face them as if they knew what was expected. And that was it. They were dancing together without having said a word. You danced by facing a girl without speaking to her, and then you moved on to dance with another girl. It was that simple. We joined in, and did the same.

Although it was exciting, I missed the physical contact

with the girls. At the disco, we did a kind of Indian war dance, but we didn't touch or hold the girls. Father Doyle had made that very clear at the beginning. There was to be no 'slow' dancing with couples holding each other. In any case, it never occurred to us to do such a thing. Girls were still remote creatures, belonging more or less to a different species. To me, girls were pure and meek like the Blessed Virgin Mary. I was soon to discover that this was not strictly accurate. Girls had other things on their minds.

A few weeks later, something extraordinary happened. I received two letters. At first I thought they might be for Da as we shared the same name, but 'Junior' was written clearly on the envelope. It wasn't my birthday which was the only time I received mail. One was a blue envelope and the other pink. The handwriting was different on each, but my name and address were neatly written on both. I went into my bedroom, hiding the letters from Ma and my brother, and opened them. They were Valentine cards. I couldn't believe it! There were kisses everywhere on both cards, and nice little drawings of flowers, but no coded message of any sort, and no names. I opened and closed the cards a dozen times, smelled them, and held them as if I could feel the fingerprints of whoever had sent them. But there were still no clues. I went into the bathroom and looked at myself in Da's shaving mirror. Normally, I only saw what was wrong: blackheads, pimples or jam on my mouth. Now I saw a round face with blue eyes and - as everyone said - my Grandma's nose. My hair was light brown with a reddish tinge at the fringe. A bit chubby-cheeked? I couldn't say. All I knew was that I had received two Valentine cards. I felt fantastic, proud, and a bit relieved; I was normal! My head was spinning. Who had sent them? It didn't matter. What mattered was that I had received them. Someone out there liked me. I must be handsome. Wait till I tell my pals, I thought! I felt like a film star!

That day I sat at my desk radiating happiness. Duffy had also received a couple of Valentine cards, which was to be expected as he was probably the best-looking boy in the class. Hogie and Mintsy had received nothing, which made them grouchy and jealous all day. 'Survival of the fittest', I thought, as I sat imagining the admiring eyes that were surely upon me. Two little cards had transformed me into a smug Narcissus. Surely the priest was wrong when he thundered against our 'earthly vanities'. No, this was a wonderful feeling. The whole world had changed. I was beginning to notice girls, and more importantly, they were noticing me.

During my last year at primary school we were sent to a different school. We had to take a bus to Dennistoun near the centre of Glasgow. I found myself in a class with lots of kids I didn't know. To my dismay, Ann Bolan was no longer in my class, but she was quickly replaced in my affections by a tall attractive girl with long fair hair. Her name was Lucy Parker, and everyone admired her, even the girls, because she had style. I soon discovered that Lucy - like most of the girls - was a lot more mature than me.

There were a couple of boys who annoyed us with their

pushiness. One of them, Alec Fraser, was small, but confident and cocky, making him seem older than his years.
One day I saw him in the playground holding up some
photos to a crowd of boys who were all hooting with
laughter. I joined the crowd and craned my neck to see
what was happening. The photos were from a photo machine, a line of four, and I couldn't believe what I saw.
Lucy Parker was passionately kissing Alec Fraser in the
photo booth! I was shocked! Kissing was for adults. I had
seen it in films with Elizabeth Taylor and Richard Burton.
Girls weren't supposed to kiss. I was bewildered. I looked
at Lucy in class afterwards. She didn't look at Alec or
speak to him, and she answered the teacher's questions
politely and modestly. How could she have done such a
thing?

Apart from two or three pecks on the cheek from
Auntie Kathleen, I had no memory of ever having been
kissed. Neither Netty, nor Peggy nor Ruby ever kissed me.
And neither did my Ma. Once when I was ill, aged about
five, Ma was sleeping in the afternoon, as she had got up
very early to go to her cleaning job. I climbed up beside
her as I was cold, but she turned, annoyed, and told me
to go and play. I never tried again. She never once put
her arms around me, and I assumed this was perfectly
normal. My only contact with her was rubbing her back
in the evenings to relieve her arthritis. But there was no
affection there. The first time I ever kissed was at my Confirmation. The priest put the bronze crucifix in front of
me and I put my lips to Christ's cold feet. My lips must
have been dirty because the priest wiped his feet as if I

had the plague. That didn't exactly encourage me to put my lips anywhere else.

But what I had glimpsed in the playground that day was the shape of things to come. And the course of events was to be determined by the girls. One day Duffy came to me with a big smile to tell me that I had been invited to a girl's party. Duffy had been asked first, and was told that he could bring a friend. Apparently, I was acceptable to the girl who was organising the party at her home the following Saturday. I knew some of the girls who were going, but not the ones from the Protestant school. I was excited; I had never been to a party before. But I was apprehensive as I didn't know what to expect.

Saturday arrived and there must have been about twenty of us at the party, ten girls and ten boys. I didn't know whose party it was, but I was told she was called Elizabeth. Nobody introduced me to the others. Music was playing, and there was Irn Bru, crisps and sweets on a table. Duffy had said that the parents would be back around 10 pm. Along with the other lads, I tucked into the sweets and Irn-Bru while the girls whispered excitedly amongst themselves. Then the girls sat down and told us to "take up our places". Two of the boys sat down beside two of the girls and put their arms around their shoulders. Duffy and I were perplexed, as were most of the other boys. Then one of the girls turned the lights down. Duffy elbowed me to make a move, and sat down beside one of the girls. I did the same, and found myself with a girl I didn't know. She didn't tell me her name. She simply turned to me, put her arms around my neck, and began to kiss me on the lips. I put my arms around her and closed my eyes like she had done, but soon I felt as if I was under water at the swimming pool. I couldn't breathe. Her lips were sucking the life out of me. Eventually I broke away, gasping for breath. Everyone else was still kissing their partners with great enthusiasm. Undaunted, my partner grabbed me and started kissing with renewed vigour, as if we were in a competition and we had fallen behind. I tried to look at her, but her hair had fallen over my face. Was she a vampire? Would I survive?

At last the music stopped, and the vampire stood up, patted me on the thigh, and moved to the next lad. I looked around, hoping to catch Duffy's eye, but suddenly there was another girl sitting on my lap. She put her arms around me, the music started, and I was subjected to another violent session of mouth to mouth resuscitation. This girl seemed to think my lips were sticks of chewing gum. She sucked and chewed, and I expected to see her spit out bits of shredded lip when the music stopped. I was breathing heavily, as if I had run a hundred yard sprint. Then another girl arrived, and it was someone I knew. She was called Linda, and she was in my class. She was a nice, quiet girl, and I was delighted to see that she had a nice small mouth. The music started, she pressed her lips on mine and this time I tried breathing through my nose. Thankfully it worked. I was elated. I could kiss and breathe at the same time. Her lips were cool and gentle; a great relief after the vampires. It was hard to believe that such a demure, shy girl, who never spoke in class, could be part of this kissing game. I wanted to speak, but she didn't let me. The aim seemed to be to break some kind of kissing record. So I decided to abandon all resistance. Hardly anyone spoke a word, not even when we changed partners. I felt hypnotised, powerless, but very happy.

Then the girls started dancing and singing along to the record player. They were all great dancers. I couldn't believe that I had kissed every one of them. Duffy appeared with a big grin on his face, but I was horrified; it looked like he had contracted some disease. There were large red blotches all over his neck. "Look in the mirror!" I told him, "You've got smallpox or something." Duffy laughed, and told me I had caught the same disease. And it was true. I went to the mirror and saw a big red mark on my neck. "It's a love-bite." Duffy said, "Don't worry. It'll go away in a few days". Good God - what were my parents going to say? Duffy had read my thoughts. "Put on your polo-neck jumper. No one will see it."

Back home, I went to the bathroom and gazed at my love-bite. Those vampire girls, I thought. I was proud of it. It was proof I had kissed and been kissed - I didn't need a photo like Alec Fraser. As soon as I was out of the Close the next morning, I took off my polo-neck, and unbuttoned my collar, to show off my trophy. Then Duffy told me that another party was planned for the following Saturday, and this time twenty girls were coming. My legs wobbled.

Many parties followed that one, all organised along the same lines. At one of these parties, a girl called Maureen invited me to go roller-skating with her and a friend at a roller-skating rink in Shettleston. She asked me to 'go with her' which meant that I had been chosen to be her boyfriend. I was flattered as she was much more mature than me, but also worried as I had never been roller-skating before. And I was right to be worried. Once on the rink I staggered about helplessly like a drunk, my legs heading in opposite directions. All around me, girls and boys were gliding along. Maureen had imagined doing the same, but instead she was stuck with me. Maybe that's why she soon stopped 'going with me'. I put it all down to experience.

Soon another girl wanted to 'go with me'. She was pretty with high cheekbones and a long graceful neck. Her hair was brushed back and she had a fringe down to her eyebrows. Her name was Christine and I had met her at the Church Disco. The first question I asked was whether she liked roller-skating. She confessed that she had never tried it, and added that she liked going to the pictures. I sighed with relief. I decided to take the plunge and to invite her on a real date. So I suggested going to the pictures and she agreed. Duffy told me that I had to impress her by taking her to a restaurant before the film. Girls liked that, he insisted. I was really apprehensive as I had never been to a restaurant. Duffy reassured me that it would be fine and said I should go to the Italian restaurant in Chambers Street just beside the cinema. His dad had taken him there. I would love it.

The meal was a disaster. The restaurant was empty apart from us. There was a stuffy atmosphere, dreadful piped xylophone music and neither of us could think of anything to say. In fact, I'd never really spoken to her before. At the disco I had danced with her a few times, and at the party the previous week she had given me a thirty-minute kiss, leaving me literally speechless. The waiter was creepy. He put on a big grin, and came to take our order, addressing me as 'Sir'. I ordered the only thing I recognised on the menu - and which was within my paper round budget - spaghetti bolognese. What a mistake. I soon learned that first dates and spaghetti bolognese don't go well together. I tried twirling the fork around the slippery mess of spaghetti but the sauce dripped all over. Soon my white shirt was splattered with tomato sauce. It looked like I had been shot. It got even worse when I tried to break the heavy silence. Slobbering spaghetti and talking at length about Celtic, is not, it would seem, the best way to charm a girl.

Fortunately, there was still the cinema. We were twelve years old and so we chose the big new Disney film, *The Jungle Book*. It was magical. Sitting in big comfortable seats with Christine's hand in mine, I was entranced by the images of the jungle; the sleek panther Bagheera, and the suave tiger, Shere Khan. I brimmed over with happiness as we watched Baloo singing *The Bare Necessities*.

I caught Christine's eye and she was radiant, too. Perhaps it was the Disney effect, but coming out of the cinema, I felt elated. We took the bus back to Easterhouse. It was Saturday night, and all the drunks were singing. We had gone from one jungle to another.

I saw Christine two or three times after that, but without a Disney film or a disco, it was like being back in the Italian restaurant. We had nothing to say to each other, so we stopped meeting up. Girls were still a mystery to me. But at twelve years old, dancing with one girl then another, or kissing one then another, was like scoring goals in the game of life.

1967 was an incredible year for me. Celtic won the European Cup. I came first in my class in my final year at primary school. I started earning money for the first time, thanks to my paper round, which meant I had more independence. I received two Valentine cards, which boosted my ego. And with my newly-found confidence, I had had two girlfriends, albeit for very short periods. And most important of all - perhaps even more important than Celtic winning the Cup - I had been kissed. It felt wonderful to be held in the arms of a girl, although I had no real feelings of desire; I was still a boy. But fond kisses had now become one of the 'bare necessities' of life.

I had been Mowgli running around the Easterhouse jungle. But I had begun to change. I was growing up, and having girlfriends spelled the end of my childhood that year, at the age of twelve. Then my voice broke, puberty arrived, and I stepped out of the Dark Close.

ABOUT THE AUTHOR

So what happened to that inquisitive, resourceful little lad when he finally stepped out of the Close of his childhood? His love of reading and his thirst for knowledge, combined with a free, inclusive and subsidised education system, opened the door to a successful university career, a degree in English Literature, and then postgraduate studies. As Jim said, books were his inspiration, and his route out of the challenging environment of his childhood; books, and an indomitable spirit, which didn't recognise social boundaries.

In 1979, Jim met a visiting postgraduate student from Paris. They fell in love, and married. Jim moved to Paris in 1980, and made France his home. Jim and Joëlle have three children, who are each pursuing successful careers. In an echo of his own childhood, Jim would take them to the local library every week, and for years the kids' favourite game was playing 'librarians'.

Jim enjoyed sharing his knowledge and insights with his children, and latterly with his beloved grand-daughter, in contrast with his own experience. Passing the parcel of knowledge came naturally, and he entered the world of teaching.

Jim taught English to high school and undergraduate students at le Lycée Hoche in Versailles, one of the most prestigious schools in France. He was a popular and respected teacher, and countless tributes from his students illustrate how he inspired them, and made a lasting impression on their young minds. His students gained from his breadth of reading and from the character of the man who had been the 'wee boy' in the Dark Close, with his bike, his comics and his football. Miss Markey and Miss Savage would have been proud of him.

Printed in Great Britain
by Amazon

55866073R00112